To every teacher who wants to make every child happy.

I0795434

curriculum

noun

noun: curriculum; plural noun: curricula; plural noun: curriculums

the subjects comprising a course of study in a school or college.
"course components of the school curriculum"
synonyms: syllabus, course of study/studies, programme of study/studies, educational programme, subjects,modules;

The word **"curriculum"** began as a Latin word which means **"a race"** or **"the course of a race".**

See **Curricle**, 18th Century: from Latin **curriculum** from **currus** chariot, from **currere** to run

Source: www.google.com/dictionary

Published by

WS Education, an imprint of
World Scientific Publishing Co. Pte. Ltd.
5 Toh Tuck Link, Singapore 596224
USA office: 27 Warren Street, Suite 401-402, Hackensack, NJ 07601
UK office: 57 Shelton Street, Covent Garden, London WC2H 9HE

National Library Board, Singapore Cataloguing in Publication Data
Name(s): Sie, Siok Hui.
Title: A teacher's race course : ruminations & reflections / Sie Siok Hui.
Description: Singapore : World Scientific Publishing Co Pte Ltd, 2019. |
Includes bibliographical references.
Identifier(s): OCN 1099482391 | ISBN 978-981-12-0715-0 (hardback) |
ISBN 978-981-12-0716-7 (paperback)
Subject(s): LCSH: Teaching--Singapore. | Curriculum planning--Singapore. |
Teacher participation in curriculum planning--Singapore. | Education--Singapore. |
Sie, Siok Hui. | Teachers--Singapore.
Classification: DDC 371.102095957--dc23

Copyright © 2019 by World Scientific Publishing Co. Pte. Ltd.

All rights reserved. This book, or parts thereof, may not be reproduced in any form or by any means, electronic or mechanical, including photocopying, recording or any information storage and retrieval system now known or to be invented, without written permission from the publisher.

For photocopying of material in this volume, please pay a copying fee through the Copyright Clearance Center, Inc., 222 Rosewood Drive, Danvers, MA 01923, USA. In this case permission to photocopy is not required from the publisher.

Cover and book illustrations by Ang Jinglin, an alumna from Singapore Chinese Girls' School, and the founder of Littlewoodloft. Littlewoodloft is a stationery and lifestyle brand that celebrates that personal touch through calligraphy and watercolour.

Design lead by Corrine Ang
Design & layout by Tan Kan

Foreword by
Rosalind Heng

Supported by
Elaine Goh (Editor)
Daphne Yuan
Tan Siao Geng

Printed in Singapore

SIE SIOK HUI

A TEACHER'S RACE COURSE

RUMINATIONS & REFLECTIONS

FOREWORD

I have always enjoyed "Black Beauty", of which the horse on this cover reminds me. In many ways, this horse is apt, as it also reminds me of Miss Sie Siok Hui—loyal, courageous, noble, of great stamina and passion, yet strong-willed and sensitive.

When Miss Sie attended an interview at my school (with a newly "independent" status bestowed on it) for the position of a Mathematics teacher, my first impression of her was one of a quiet self-effacing teacher. She was young, relatively inexperienced; but I sensed a streak of tenacity, which could be obstinate. This quality proved to be a boon in her craft as a teacher and in her determination to push her pupils forward, while it was a bane to school administration who had expectations of compliant staff. She exemplifies how teaching is not just a job or a career but a vocation. Despite the advanced stage of her cancer, Miss Sie's persistence in producing this volume because she believes that her findings in her Masters research will enlighten the education community is typical of this tenacity as well.

For her pupils, Miss Sie would go that extra mile and beyond, constantly researching and carrying out different strategies to ensure her pupils understood and learnt the mathematical concepts she taught because she believed in the proper cognitive development of her pupils. This was developed into an art—she had open, transparent discussions with both pupils and fellow teachers regarding the way the scheme of work and lessons should be prepared. She was one of the rare few who did not chase after results, and yet her pupils achieved extremely impressive grades.

Today, many of her former pupils remember her for the love she had put into her relationships with them, and many became close friends with their mentor. This volume captures an example of this in the exchange of emails between Miss Sie and her one-time student, Ryan. The respect she won, illustrated in the extracts in Chapter Four, shows she was a teacher who did not just teach her subject, but was also an educator.

The chapter on her reflections on human values and tendencies indicates a wisdom acquired through a long hard journey, one which she describes as a race course. This book describes the experiences and events in the journey she embraced with determination, searching for goodness in the hearts of those she encountered, and in her strong faith in God.

For all the happy consequences she has brought to all who have walked with her, Miss Sie had indeed, not lived in vain.

Rosalind Heng

Principal

Singapore Chinese Girls' School

(1979–2006)

EDITOR'S NOTE

Sie Siok Hui and I went to the same university and read English, but never sat in the same lectures. We were even hostel mates, but never worked together, though we knew of each other, because the hostel was small—more like a village. It was only when she joined the school I was teaching in, that I had the opportunity to make her acquaintance which blossomed unexpectedly into a thirty-year-old friendship.

This is a work of love which pleads for a broader perspective of teaching as an art. Interwoven with anecdotes and reflections on her life journey, Siok Hui has also created a work of compassion with insights into the Singapore education system.

In a sensitive and frank contemplation as she nears the end of her own course of life which has been cut short by cancer, she passionately advocates a re-look at teacher training and teacher education to uplift the quality of our education system. In her inimitable candid style, she reveals her own moments of epiphany for improving her craft as a teacher. She always pushed boundaries—her own and those of institutional requirements—in order to benefit the students whom she called her "kids".

This is a must-read not only for teachers and educational leaders, but also anyone who wishes to catch a glimpse of the heart and mind of an educator who was intentional in the choice of institutions to teach in because she always wanted to know more. Hers has been a purposeful life on a road few would choose to travel.

This volume has been a work long in its incubation but breathlessly swift in its production due to the escalation of the cancer over two months. There are many who have contributed time, effort and cost without thought to themselves. I particularly wish to thank Miss Rosalind Heng for her generous foreword, Daphne Yuan and Tan Siao Geng for the countless hours of research, editing and invaluable help in the distribution of this book, Corrine Ang and Ang Jinglin for the beautiful artwork and production of this volume, and all Siok Hui's students who have given permission for their letters and emails to be re-produced.

Thank you, all.

Elaine Lim
Editor

PROLOGUE

"Curriculum" is the Latin word for "race course".

In the 1960s, Convent of the Holy Infant Jesus (CHIJ) was perhaps a more established primary school than others. Within a class of mixed-ability children, there was banding to form groups based somewhat on ability. I remember vaguely in one of the primary school years, I was seated next to a classmate who was very weak in Maths and was tasked to help her. In fact, this became a feature in Maths classes in the remaining primary school years. I helped this classmate for a few years. We then went our different ways after primary school.

Some years later, I met the mother of this classmate near my neighbourhood. She looked happy to see me and thanked me for the kindness shown to her daughter. She told me that the girl had died; she had a tumour in her brain. It dawned on us that could have been the reason for her inability that had irritated the teachers so greatly then; "stupid" was an adjective hurled in her direction not infrequently. Perhaps the "natural" teacher within me was born in my primary school classrooms.

At 16, I decided to help with the difficult financial situation at home. I thought that I could work part-time as a tutor. I offered my services to the proprietor of a neighbourhood provision shop, our family's good friend, and secured my first tutee six years younger than me. We reconnected in 2017. A very diffident and introverted girl whom I finally drew out of her shell, she became my first dear student.

This was the start of this teacher's self-training on her race course.

Teaching was destined to be in my blood, though at that time, I had vehemently denied it as I had set my heart on being a researcher of sorts. Not a teacher.

Fast forward to my Public Service Commission scholarship (PSC) interview. I had done abysmally for all my "Special" (S) papers in the GCE "A" Level Examinations, which blew my chances of an overseas merit scholarship. At the scholarship interview, I was asked, "Are you prepared to teach?" Pragmatic me replied, "Yes." I needed funds to study even locally. I would do anything to secure the funds. I was taken aback that that was the one and only question the interviewers asked about teaching. I wondered if the aptitude for teaching and the attitude towards teaching were assumed. On the basis of that one answer alone, I came to be bonded to the teaching service for six years. Pragmatism ruled!

Thus, a teacher was "accidentally" made.

Sie Siok Hui

CONTENTS

PART II DEFINING THE RACE COURSE

PART 1

Voices of Meandering

To add value to others, one must first value others.

John C. Maxwell

CHAPTER 1
OF VALUES AND VALUATION

The tradition of returning to our alma mater to visit the school and teachers is still prevalent, I am sure, in most schools—albeit due to security reasons and the wish not to interrupt lessons—it is probably confined to special days like Teachers' Day or festive occasions. We hardly ask ourselves why we do so; it is probably mostly due to nostalgia, a part of ourselves in our childhood and teenage years being inextricably bound to the school, or a sense of belonging. It has to be the good vibes...yet behind all that, my view is that the invisible hand here is values—a sense of not only what is good, but also what is appreciated. The way that this is expressed need not necessarily be confined to physical visits to the school or teachers. In the present age, with the ubiquitous use of social media and other means to maintain links with ease, students are no longer limited to mere cards and letters. The values they have assimilated can be displayed through the bonds built through the years such as inviting their teachers to their weddings, bringing their children to school to introduce the little ones to their mummy's or daddy's teacher or even extending their relationships beyond that of teacher-student relationships to personal friendships.

> ***She did not ask more than I was willing to share and merely listened to me. Yet, she seemed to completely understand what I was going through.***

I ask myself how these values may be measured or weighed; when a school is evaluated, the values which have been assimilated by its students are not part of the evaluation process. There is a tendency to value visible outcomes like students' academic results because these can be accredited and honoured as a tangible form of evaluation. We likewise habitually evaluate students based on visible outcomes, be it academic or co-curricular activities, or success in competitions, for the same reasons. Yet, as educators, how do we weigh the worth of a student? Or, to consider it another way, how do we define a valuation of any student? Although I have always felt that there is a lot more to the word "valuation" than just "evaluation", it was only in recent years that I have been able to crystallise my thoughts. Let me illustrate this anecdotally.

ANECDOTE 1

When I was in Primary Six, groups of ex-students interrupted our lessons when they visited my teachers. They were almost always laughing and telling the teachers of their new secondary school experiences. At that time, I looked forward to graduating from primary school so that I could visit my teachers in a similar fashion. I admit now, what was uppermost in my mind, was probably a sense of self-importance, that I was "grown-up". I could have made similar group visits after I left my primary school, though I have no recollection of them. In any case, access to school was never an issue, since it was only a short walk across a road and it was also within a church compound and therefore open even on weekends.

But I definitely recall one particular visit to an exceptional teacher, Miss Daisy Wee. During that visit to Miss Wee, I confided that I had difficulty adjusting to my new secondary school environment and felt bewildered. She did not ask more than I was willing to share and merely listened to me. Yet, she seemed to completely understand what I was going through and perceptively identified the source of my anxieties, tracing it to the difficulties I had had at home from young. This helped me very much to understand myself. To this day, I remember her words and my gratitude towards her for her empathy. In that short time with her after I graduated from primary school, she had done what she regarded as only her duty as a teacher. Unbeknownst to her however, her kindness and perception had helped a very sensitive maladjusted child see hope in her little sad world. This teacher touched my life profoundly.

It took me 30 years or so before I understood why she meant so much to me. It is always easy to say, "She is nice, caring, etc." There always were nice teachers; but not all nice teachers left an impact. She was probably the only teacher who valued me or made me feel I was valued, and the one teacher who made the deepest impact in my life. I was not exactly a well-liked student, not being the typical 乖 (obedient) student, despite being recognised as intelligent. While all the other teachers mercilessly labelled me as a "talkative" girl throughout my primary school years and consistently wrote this in my report book as the only remark they could make on my performance as a student, she looked past all the complaints and made me a prefect, gave me the chance to be part of the level Chinese dance and entrusted me with other responsibilities. Hers was the best year I had in primary school life and the only year without any negative adjectives in my report book. I made it a point as a teacher never to commit a similar offence against *any* child!

ANECDOTE 2

When it was my turn to be an educator, I had my fair share of visits from past students. Even though the visits came at the expense of time with my present students, I liked to find out how and what my graduated students were doing. In 1990, some of the students from the previous year came to visit me. They were from a very weak class who had only been allowed to do a seven-subject combination: Elementary Mathematics, Human and Social Biology (which was not considered a Science subject), Art, Religious Studies, the two languages and Geography. I never liked the subject combination as it left the students with very few options after secondary school. Some of the subjects were easier to score in but had little value to the students after graduation. The class had had a number of disciplinary issues but they were not bad at all. Thankfully, they all passed my subject, Elementary Maths, fairly well. During that visit, I remember asking how a particular student was doing, and why she was not with them. One of her classmates mentioned that she was working. She had said she was not doing well anyway, and therefore did not see any point in returning to see her teachers. That hit me very hard. I have never forgotten that moment, even to this day some 29 years later. I will never forget the disappointment and sadness I had felt.

I want to see my kids because they had been my kids.

I want to see my students do well. But this is not the reason I want to see them. I want to see my kids because they had been my kids. I value every one of them, whether they achieved straight "A"s or they failed. It does not matter. Each of them is a human being, a person worthy of value. Thereafter, I remember telling every batch of students that I wanted them to return to visit me. I wanted to know how each of them was getting on, regardless of their results or what they were doing. I emphasised that they mattered to me. I hope that this point had hit home for at least some of them.

I had therefore felt the disappointment keenly because I felt the reasons given by that student who had not visited me stems from society's general definition of success and that I had failed her in not assuring her of her worth as a person. By always emphasising good results, I had inadvertently reinforced society's message myself, though I definitely value each child. I definitely cared for this child and her welfare and really wanted to know how she was doing. But I realised, with dismay, that I had not given this as much emphasis as I ought while she had been in school. I always reflect on this with regret and so from then on, consciously made the effort to reassure struggling students that they mattered more than the results. To this day, I remember this child who had taught me this precious lesson on valuation.

It is part of our culture to praise students who have attained many distinctions. But among those who had fallen short of the mark, did they all put in less effort than those who had scored well? How often success obfuscates effort! A student whose parent is a surgeon shared that her father had felt that the hardest thing to him was to face the patient's family's looks of distress and grief when a surgery did not go well. Does a surgeon put in less effort in a surgery that went awry? Very seldom do we validate effort over outcome. I do not dispute that the outcome is almost always a determining factor of "success"; however, "success" is a word I mentally discard because when assessing for "success", the idea of valuation is not part of the definition. To me, a person's worth and efforts are to be far more valued than what "success" could possibly represent.

As teachers, every child is to be valued. Every. Child. Valued.

To me, "valuation" is to see the value of every child, to love the person as he is. As teachers, every child is to be valued. Every. Child. Valued.

ANECDOTE 3

During my adjunct teaching in a neighbourhood school in 2005–2006, I experienced a poignant encounter. I had returned to the school to see how the students had fared when the "O" level results had been released. Generally, most of them had done fairly well, especially in Maths. There would always be casualties, though thankfully, there were not many that year. Most of the students were happy and excitedly planning the next phase in life and they came forward to thank the teachers. Towards the later part of the afternoon I was walking along the corridor on my way out of the school, when I met a student leader from a uniformed group who had been waiting for me. He came up to me saying, "I'm so sorry, I should have listened to you." The moment that he apologised, I felt very much for him. This encounter had greater impact on me than all the thanks I had received from the students who had done well. To this day, this personal confession that afternoon is the only thing I remember. While I was happy for all the students who had done well, I hold dear such students who showed personal growth during my time with them. I especially cherish this boy's apology for not realising his potential for the fact that he had waited outside the school just to express that to me. From before, I had told him I believed in him and his ability but that

When we praise certain people for their achievements, is there not an implication that those without achievements are somewhat lacking?

hard work and discipline was indispensable and could overcome weaknesses. After his apology, I had encouraged him to continue to pursue his dreams, told him that he had leadership potential as seen in his uniformed group achievements and that he could go very far in this field. I should have established a point of contact before we parted. Regrettably, I had not.

Our focus is too often on the results or the achievements. When we praise certain people for their achievements, is there not an implication that those without achievements are somewhat lacking? Do not wait until a child "fails" before telling him that you love him even if he does not reach those end goals. Unconditional love should be expressed all the time. I hope every teacher (and parent) realises the innate value of each child and that his journey is more important than the destination.

Education is about values. I never felt I belaboured that point with all my kids sufficiently. But so long as one child remembers, being an educator (not a teacher) has not been in vain.

ANECDOTE 4

Twenty-four years ago, in 1994, one of my graduating classes had to decide where to pose for the informal class photograph. The school's motto, "Sincerity, Courage, Generosity, Service", stood out boldly on each of the four walls in the concourse. Though it was over 20 years ago, I distinctly recall saying, "Let's take our class photo with the word 'Courage', for in life's journey, you will need a lot of courage."

COURAGE

Twenty years later, in 2014, I heard this exact story recounted by one of my former students, Chiyin, in her acceptance speech for an award conferred on her. I cannot describe that swell of emotion when I realised how a fleeting moment 20 years back had left a small but definite mark on the life of a young lady who is an internationally acclaimed photographer today. More importantly, she is a young lady who has been beating a pathway through unknown territory to be a voice for the unheard, to tell the story of those who cannot do so themselves. The Guest of Honour had commented to me: "You must be very proud of her." I had paused

> *"Let's take our class photo with the word 'Courage', for in life's journey, you will need a lot of courage."*

momentarily. I could not honestly agree with that statement. After some thought, I replied that I was proud of Chiyin for who she was, not because of the award.

Anyone who knows me well would know I avoid social functions, especially those with some degree of aggrandisement. I only attended Chiyin's award ceremony because she had said it would mean a lot to her. It was for her sake, for her as the person I had known 20 years ago and whose journey I had kept up with from afar. That she had gained international recognition is not the point. I value Chiyin as a person, just as any of my students deserve to be valued. I had respected her from the day she started fighting for the rights of migrant workers as a journalist, long before she started winning awards. I respect her still for choosing to dedicate her life and her gifts to the service of humanity, not without cost to herself.

She remembered values. This is the essence of education.

After that suggestion from the Guest of Honour, I reflected on what makes me proud of my kids. I know I was very proud to be at all the recitals put up by my kids through the years. I know I was very proud to attend the art exhibitions that displayed their works. I know they poured their hearts and lives into their work. I know I was very proud to attend the passing out parade of the boys because they had completed a milestone in their lives and were transitioning into adulthood. I know I have always been very proud of my kids who contact me and tell me of how they are doing, especially those who had shown resilience in overcoming obstacles. I know I am happy when I read internet posts of kids reflecting and growing in depth of thought and character. It is these personal moments and not the moments of glory in achieving "success" as defined by society. That is merely peripheral.

Despite agreeing to be in attendance at Chiyin's moment of success, I had actually regretted my decision upon reaching the award ceremony venue. The need to be "sociable" never sits well with me. However, her speech had made all the difference to my life as an educator. It was not because of the gratitude she expressed toward me but because she had defined what I truly believe about education. She remembered values. This is the essence of education. She had remembered the motto of her school and her meaningful journey in education in those years that had been the source of her care and concern for humanity. My own primary school had also taught me well. I will never forget the school motto—"Simple in Virtue, Steadfast in Duty" and the words "noblesse oblige" engraved on our school badge. These are the values that I live by.

A ship in
harbour is safe,
but that is
not what ships are
built for.

John A. Shedd

CHAPTER 2
A LEARNING RACE COURSE: LEARNING AND TEACHING

In school, I failed my art...without fail! In art lessons, we were given a title and then expected to draw. For me, it was always somehow a house, a stick diagram and then after that, I never quite got anything correct. We were merely given materials to complete the art assignment; there was no "teaching" of techniques to perform the task. Lacking direction and natural artistic flair, my artwork was often the butt of rather cruel jokes. Unfortunately, creating art was not my only weakness.

I realised much later also, that I had poor hand-eye coordination and was possibly slightly dyslexic. I always had difficulties recognising left shoes from right shoes which infuriated my mother. When I was young, my sister could play the piano, draw, swim and dance. I was not able to hit a shuttlecock; I could not co-ordinate my hands when I read piano notes; and when I had to march, my hands and legs did not synchronise well. It could have been overcome with practice and encouragement; however, I belonged to a different era. Perhaps all these painful learning difficulties helped me to be a better and more sensitive teacher.

My generation was a generation where emphasis was placed on the negatives—what you could not do was always highlighted. There were, however, other things that I could do. During my time in school, I was considered an academically strong student yet somehow praise never came my way. I went on to do well enough to get into University with a Teaching Bursary that determined my pathway in life.

It was one very painful experience that was perhaps the determining factor in my attitude to teaching. Due to many extenuating circumstances, within the family, in the over-involvement in co-curricular activities at the University as well as difficult personal relationships, I repeated a year in the University. My bursary was suspended. It was a very bitter year in my life; with very little support, it was very hard for someone of about 21 years of age. However, that experience taught me what it was like to be at rock-bottom. I never saw students who failed in the same way after this. I knew then what it was like to be where they were, a feeling I admit I never knew before. When I finally embarked on my teaching pathway, I wanted to teach in the

Perhaps all these painful learning difficulties helped me to be a better and more sensitive teacher.

Normal Stream. I wanted to be where the weak students were. However, I was assigned to an all-girls Express Stream school. I regarded it as Providence.

Fifteen years in the education service, the passing of my late father nine years after a stroke and many personal traumatic circumstances, caused me to be in a burnt-out state. I felt I had to resign from my beloved career to recuperate and sort myself out. It was a very painfully deliberate decision but a necessary move at the time. Thereafter, I led a somewhat reclusive life.

During this painful "down time", I sought constructive outlets to "vent" the complex feelings that I was experiencing and to occupy my mind. It was during this period that I started to pick up some hobbies, and in the process, fulfilled some of my childhood dreams.

Knitting was the first hobby I tried out. I was inspired by the scriptural verse in the Bible, Colossians 2:2,

> *"...that their hearts might be comforted, being* ***knit*** *together in love, and unto all riches of the full assurance of understanding, to the acknowledgement of the mystery of God, and of the Father, and of Christ..."*

I was curious why the word "knit" was used, and what its application should mean among the Christian brethren. For months, there were days when I knit day and night, till my fingers ached. The knit and purl interwove together beautifully to form a finished product. I knit socks for my mother, a scarf for a very dear friend from my school-days and a cushion for my favourite principal. However, till today, I am still none the wiser regarding how knitting relates to the comforting of hearts among Christians!

Next, music. I never thought I would ever learn to play the piano. However, I loved music and wanted some music in my life. I started with the Chinese flute and I managed to learn a few tunes. Later in 2004, I wanted to purchase a small keyboard to play. By a stroke of luck, somebody traded in her Clavinova for a piano at the Yamaha shop I patronised, so I bought it. To make good use of it, I thought I should sign up for lessons for a few months. This was how I met one of the best teachers in my life, Chris. Months stretched into years, and I ended up taking lessons for nine years under her.

...she had read me well, so she had pushed me to surmount the steep learning curve; in the process, I learnt much about learning in my areas of weakness and how to overcome them.

When I was eight years old, my very first piano teacher had told my mother that I would not be able to play the piano well. I can understand why. I had difficulty co-ordinating the fingers of my two hands and co-ordinating between my hands and my feet. I struggled between counting and playing the keys, between pedalling and playing and between reading notes and playing. I was also sensitive to the teacher's impatience. Once I sensed that the teacher was irritated with me due to my "stupidity" and lack of progress, my mind would freeze and I would lose confidence. As a teacher, my personal experience of such debilitating feelings helped me empathise with students who struggle with academic work.

Chris, on the other hand, provided me with an alternative experience. She was wonderful—very patient, practical, and encouraging. Not once did she appear impatient, exasperated, or condescending. Initially, I told her I did not want to take exams and that I would be happy just to play a few songs. However, after two years, she convinced me to take the Associated Board of the Royal Schools of Music (ABRSM) Grade Three Practical Examinations, which I passed with distinction. Later, I also passed the Grades Five and Six Practical Examinations, to my immense jubilation. Those who are musically-inclined, talented, and dexterous can never imagine how challenging it is for an older person with

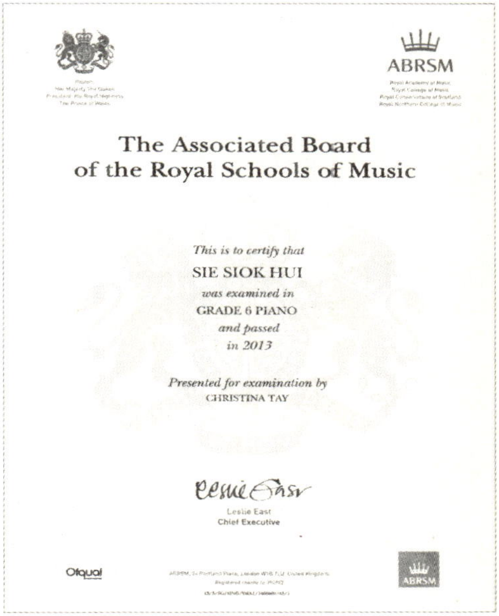

ABRSM

The Associated Board
of the Royal Schools of Music

This is to certify that
SIE SIOK HUI
was examined in
GRADE 6 PIANO
and passed
in 2013

Presented for examination by
CHRISTINA TAY

Leslie East
Chief Executive

Ofqual

ABRSM

little sense of rhythm and poor hand-eye coordination, to scale such a huge mountain. It was a significant milestone for me; it provided me with a new narrative about overcoming tremendous odds. It was also another lesson to teach my students. Why Chris had encouraged me to take the examinations was because she had felt I needed to be more disciplined in picking up techniques and to be more precise with the phrasing. She saw my weaknesses and felt that I could achieve a level of competency if I had targets. In this, she had read me well, so she had pushed me to surmount the steep learning curve; in the process, I learnt much about learning in my areas of weakness and how to overcome them. Sitting that Grade Three Examination was a victory in learning. Not the results.

Around the same time that I was learning the piano, I decided to learn how to draw too, partly because I never quite believed that I was totally unable to draw. As a Maths teacher, no matter how weak my students were, I told them everyone could do a bit of Maths. It is not possible to be totally no good. Besides, I remember a very good Art teacher saying to me, had she taught me, she would have been able to help me to draw. Hence, when I had the time, I told myself, "Let me look for an art teacher and try it out". By chance, I found one, Ms Le Man, from Harbin, China. I took to her and was under her tutelage for six months.

I also started to make sketches. Ms Le Man was a lively lady who was full of zest; she was always open and spontaneous, talented and patient. An excellent teacher, she only taught me for six months, yet managed to nurture some artistic skills in me, which had previously been non-existent. When I produced the sketches below, I was in such disbelief that I had to ask myself, "Who drew these?" I had felt so proud and unashamedly admired my own work for days.

These sketches were proof that I could be taught to draw; they were physical manifestations of my overcoming a mental obstacle and realising a dream. No one can ever know what these sketches mean to me—a "confirmed failure" in art.

Sketch of a Peacock (Aug 2004)

I was unable to keep away from teaching for long, and gradually returned to it by way of relief teaching and then adjunct teaching. I was finally back in the teaching profession. It was also then that I felt it was time to embark on a Master of Education. I had always wanted to pursue it but circumstances had never been favourable. Besides, to make the long journey to the National Institute of Education (NIE) on public transport would have been too arduous. Although I had learnt to drive in my twenties, I had not passed the test. I knew my poor co-ordination and poor sense of direction would stand in the way of my getting a driving licence, but by now, I was conscious of my disabilities and I knew how to use my strengths to overcome my weaknesses. I was determined to give it a good try. Safe driving was of paramount importance to me, hence I engaged a very good instructor

Sketch of a Savannah Sparrow (2004)

and put in 120 hours of practice; I passed my driving test within six months. Again, for those who know of my weaknesses, this was a major achievement—one that even my mother was immensely proud of.

Let me share a final learning experience. Anyone who has almost drowned will know how traumatising it is to attempt to swim again. I was eleven and had attended a classmate's birthday party. She had a swimming pool at her house, and I had not realised the pool was not uniform in depth throughout. I was hardly a swimmer to begin with, so I had never been able to breathe correctly when I was learning the breast stroke some time earlier. I did not tell my parents that I would be swimming. I really should not have gone into the pool. Before I knew it, I was in a part of the pool which was too deep for me to stand and breathe; I was unable to come up for breath, yet I kept gasping for air in the water and trying to get help by grasping at swimmers who swam past above me as I sank into the waters. I remember being resigned to dying and lost consciousness. I think this probably saved me, because it helped me to float. Thankfully, my classmate's father had realised something was amiss and I was pulled out of the water unconscious, but alive. The next thing I remember was opening my eyes, seeing

> ***...it is only when you have to struggle with personal handicaps and inner obstacles that you are able to truly empathise with students who have their own hurdles to learning.***

faces around me, and calling out my friends' names to let them know that I was conscious and alive! I was very much traumatised by the experience but dared not tell anyone at home for fear of punishment. This close brush with death weighed heavily on my soul.

Subsequently in later years, I tried to learn swimming from friends. Whether it was my psychological state or my body frame that somehow did not float easily, none of my friends succeeded in helping me to swim. More recently in 2013, I was diagnosed with spondylosis. I was encouraged by my physician to take up swimming as it is a good exercise for the back. In a conversation with my classmate, she had shared that her mother had started learning to swim at the age of sixty. I had thought to myself, "If she can do it, why can't I?" I had not needed cajoling; I had just needed to see the reason why. Once that had clicked into place and the will set, these were all I needed to move into action. There must have been a cognitive acceptance and an affective affirmation.

My first instructor had not been too helpful. I then decided to engage my former student whom I knew to be a competent instructor and learnt humility by taking instruction from him. Suffice to say that after two years, I was able to accomplish both the breast and freestyle strokes and at my peak, my practice swim comprised 10 lengths of the pool. Again, what seemed like an insignificant accomplishment to some, was a great milestone to me. I celebrated this process of overcoming not only an area of weakness, but also a childhood nightmare. The dark shadow was finally gone; in its place was an inner victory.

My various experiences in overcoming my weaknesses have

affirmed this belief: it makes you a better teacher to learn something that you are not good at, or lack interest in, or have some innate fear of. My first piece of wisdom learnt was that it is only when you have to struggle with personal handicaps and inner obstacles that you are able to truly empathise with students who have their own hurdles to learning. Secondly, no matter how determined a student you are, you need a good instructor or teacher to guide you to overcome your weaknesses. A good teacher will understand your fears in learning, point out your blind spots, encourage you to overcome obstacles along the way and motivate you to reach greater heights. I will never be a pianist of great accomplishment, nor a driver with great dexterity. Yet, I would never have been able to achieve what I have without my teachers. All teachers, whatever discipline they teach in, should aspire to be good teachers of the above calibre.

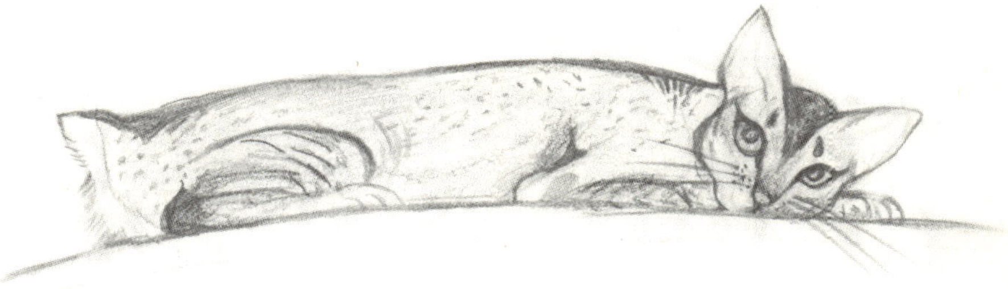

Sketch of my cat, Brownee (Nov 2004)

Sketch of my cat, Tiger (Dec 2004)

Experience is a double-edged sword.

CHAPTER 3
TEACHING AND LEARNING: COGNITIVE DEVELOPMENT AND LEARNER AWARENESS

When teaching takes place, does it ensure learning takes place? I started out early in my life as a tutor and was relatively good at it. Likewise, my relief teaching stints always affirmed my ability to teach. To me, the delivery of lessons in an interesting manner was teaching.

The first school I was assigned to, I was not the teacher that the school actually needed. I was trained in English and Mathematics. It was their Geography teacher who was leaving for further studies. They did not need an English or Maths teacher. However, one of their senior Maths teachers had medical issues with her pregnancy which required her to take a few weeks' medical leave. I was therefore assigned to relief-teach in her Secondary Four Additional Mathematics and Physics classes. I was unfazed. I got hold of the content and did my best to deliver. This was teaching, wasn't it? It was expected of any teacher at that time. Whatever work you were given to do by the administration, you just did it.

After this, I was assigned to teach seven Secondary One Geography classes, one English class, one Maths class and one Physical Education class. This disparate lot of subjects was given in order to fill up my time-table. I did it. That was expected of anyone in teaching. Surprisingly, I found teaching the topic of significant figures in Secondary One Maths quite difficult. It was so easy to explain, but somehow it was so hard for the students to grasp. But the kids were very sweet. They just repeated after me, "0.00001 is one significant figure!" and enjoyed the loud choral response. However, I knew not much had sunk in.

I received good feedback from the Secondary Four classes that I had earlier taught as a relief teacher and I was thus tasked the following year to teach Additional Mathematics in Upper Secondary. I was really glad. I had always known that I related better to the content in the Upper Secondary level. It was teaching at this level that I discovered that there was much to learn in the technique of solving questions. I remember coming across a question that I could not solve, so I had asked a senior Maths teacher for help. I had also asked her why she could solve it whereas I could not. All she said was, "Experience. If you solve enough questions, you would know." I was a very diligent teacher, so I took her words literally and did every

Students at a certain cognitive level have similar difficulties.

single question in the textbook and ten-year series. In fact, I got to know the different textbooks available so well that I knew which text had good questions for any particular topic.

My first four years in teaching two cycles of Upper Secondary Maths would be considered an enviable success: the pass rate was 100%, with above 70% distinctions and hardly any below the "B" grade. It was achieved through a lot of hard work, especially with the weaker students. In those days, there were hardly any students whom we would say had "attitude" problems, at least not in the school I taught. However, there were classes that were distinctly weaker academically. My solution was having many remediation hours. I had also been told earlier that if a student did not understand a method, I must try to explain it in a different way. I had difficulty with this because I did not know how. I only knew that I could be patient and repeat myself over and over, breaking down the concepts and explaining them step by step. Whatever it was, both the hard work by the students and my dogged determination paid off, as the results showed. I was personally stunned by my success and I admit that I took pride in this achievement.

During this period, there were four distinct experiences which led to reflections that left a deep imprint on me.

The first experience was teaching trigonometric graphs at Secondary Three. I was quite upset that the students could not follow my instructions for drawing good graphs. I was certain it was due to their attentiveness. What I noticed however, in my next cycle of teaching Secondary Three two years later, was that the group of students also had the same issue. This was when the concept of cognitive readiness first occurred to me. Students at a certain cognitive level have similar difficulties. I also observed that somehow, some of these issues were resolved when they reached Secondary Four. I was to get acquainted with the word "cognition" later in my life. "Cognition" is a term referring to the mental processes involved in gaining knowledge and comprehension. These processes include thinking, knowing, remembering, judging and problem-solving. I realised early on, that one of my roles as a teacher was to facilitate the development of these mental processes in students, so that they would be able to apply them independently and effectively.

The second experience arose from a remark shared by the senior Maths teacher. Her husband was then a head of department in another school where the principal demanded compulsory remedial classes be held. He had said to her that when a teacher had to hold so many remedial sessions, was he remediating the students' learning, or remediating his teaching? At that time, I was well-known in the school for conducting remediation sessions relentlessly. I was taken aback by that statement and felt it warranted a lot of soul-searching. Did I teach well in the first place? I realised that teaching long hours and working hard did not equate to teaching well.

I received feedback from a colleague that some of my Maths students found me to be sarcastic and extremely results-oriented in my teaching. I knew the first round of success had led me to join a numerical chase which I hated myself. However, the results were important to the students (in those days there was no school ranking and no one tracked results except myself—or at least that was what I thought—for no one ever complimented me on my track record in the school. My way of working was not well received, to put it mildly.) I felt I needed to break away from that bondage of chasing results so I applied for a nine-month part-time course ran by the British Council—the Royal Society of Arts (RSA) Teaching English in Secondary School offered by the University of Cambridge. This was one of the turning points of my teaching career.

In 1990, I completed this highly demanding and rigorous course which taught me a lot about pedagogical planning. In a term of 10 weeks, there were six observation lessons. My tutors were very critical. In the observations, my lesson plans were tracked by the minute: "You are 10 minutes behind ... 20 minutes behind...". I was ambitious, so I did a module on Comprehension using the newspapers but misjudged the way the students would respond, so the lesson went awry. "Why are you teaching Comprehension?" was the question one tutor had continually peppered me with. He had refused to accept the reason that it was an examination requirement. This had made me think. Another tutor who saw how my never-ending Maths marking took up so much of my time, questioned my teaching methodology. I was paranoid about marking as I felt that this was the only way that I could ensure my students had done their work, and it was the way to find out what they did or did not know. It was very effective as I could

...when a teacher had to hold so many remedial sessions, was he remediating the students' learning, or remediating his teaching?

track every student well, though it was at the expense of an enormous amount of time and energy. I became exhausted. I did eventually reconsider my whole approach when my pedagogical skills were enhanced.

I had never been comfortable with role-play as a teaching strategy and was quite resistant to it. However, an activity that I learnt in the RSA course sorted out my bias against it. I discovered that involving students in role-plays allowed them to be totally immersed in the topic, which then promoted student engagement in learning. I realised that this is vital in every learning process. It was also through one of the tutors, Ms Wynne Cline, that I came across the concept of Error Analysis. Analysing errors in the compositions of students can help teachers trace the deeper issues which cause common problems. For example, I did a phonological error analysis of my own pronunciation in a reading of a passage and discovered that there was much interference from my Chinese dialect which had affected my articulation. I did many recordings to rectify my diction and bravely took on my final diploma project in this area, working with my students on phonology. It was a very fruitful adventure and I realised that learner awareness is essential to activate the cognitive to develop. And it first starts with teacher awareness. The teacher is the key to facilitate this

I realised then that there is no such thing as a total lateral transfer of teaching pedagogical skills when moving from one set of students to another.

learning process. I found the strategies acquired in the Diploma course so very relevant that I transferred these pedagogical skills to the realm of Maths teaching.

The third experience involved another level of learning which took place when I joined an independent school in 1991. The school embraced a ten-year school system where one Principal takes care of the Primary and Secondary schools. The heart of the Principal was magnanimous as she advocated for students who enrolled from the age of seven in the school being given a complete ten-year education so long as they qualified for the Express stream. Thus, this school accepted students with a wide range of PSLE scores from 200–270 and above. As a result, a wider repertoire of pedagogical strategies needed to be employed.

The initial two years of adjustment were not smooth. Although the previous school at which I had taught and this one were both all-girls schools, the way the students learned Maths was quite different. In the first school, the students were more diffident, more compliant towards instruction and very willing to attempt whatever homework dished out so that the practice resulted in subsequent good performance. In this second school, the students were more confident and articulate, much more humanities-inclined and not too fond of Maths as a subject, and so my instructional approaches were not well received. I realised then that there is no such thing as a total lateral transfer of teaching pedagogical skills when moving from one set of students to another. The learners' profile, their inclinations and the Maths foundation they have are factors that must all be considered in planning for a lesson. I was determined to address these issues.

As the school had been conferred an "independent" status, there was a certain amount of freedom given to us to design our lessons. One of the concessions given to us was a 10% assessment component for us to assess our students' learning in any way we deemed appropriate. It was through this that I experimented with a "graded" exercise which proved to be very effective as a simple check on whether learning had taken place. This sharp instrument I have introduced to every school I subsequently joined and strongly advocate the use of it. Whilst it sounds simple, it can be surprising how few teachers use it effectively. My chief contention for why this happens is that they are more preoccupied with achievement as signified by marks than whether learning takes place. One is not equivalent to the other.

I have found that a very important way of understanding how to teach from different angles is to learn from the minds of textbook writers. The sequencing of concepts taught differs in the minds of different teachers. This shows that there are many approaches a teacher can take; depending on the prior knowledge of the students, the different abilities of students and the amount of the material to cover, teachers can adopt different strategies. I had mentioned I did not know how to remediate using different strategies in my early years as a teacher but I soon acquired the art by diligently studying different textbooks, and not only local ones at that. I was amazed at how much I learnt by just doing the exercises and following the writer's intent and principles in his content design of the textbook. Some books are written for students to work through and learn while most local textbooks are meant for teachers to use for instruction.

Having learnt so much from the writers of textbooks, whenever I teach a new concept, I would design a worksheet that covers the key points. The last 10 minutes of the lesson would be set aside for students to attempt the worksheet. They were permitted to refer to their notes or to me, but not to their friends. Some questions were just exact replicas of the type of question taught in the lesson. The idea is to check if learning takes place. When a student stares at it and can hardly write, there are two reasons. The student was not with you at all in the lesson, or the student is so paralysed by inertia and the lack of confidence, that he cannot start. You can read the many different states of mind from the way the students attempt the exercise.

Concepts must be layered in and connected to help students learn during concept-building.

I must confess that I have very often found the "creative" and "innovative" stance in lesson design of recent years has not helped in laying a firm foundation for a strong conceptual approach. It is not unusual to see challenging questions appearing mid-way in the scheme of work since the "basic" concepts are supposedly easy to grasp. Many teachers make the mistake of designing tough worksheets which defeats the purpose of this instrument. In the interests of time, rather than creating their own questions, some teachers extract challenging questions from textbooks because they are trying to expose their students to as many types of questions as possible. The intent is laudable—in the likelihood that any of these questions appear in the national examinations, the students would know how to solve them. However, textbook writers, especially for Mathematics, tend to sequence content in a manner that builds new understanding on prior knowledge. Without the prior knowledge which the textbook writer had in mind when he set a question, the students are unlikely to have competency in the subject matter, much less mastery of the concept, to produce an acceptable answer. Concepts must be layered in and connected to help students learn during concept-building. Unless students master basic concepts well, requiring them to work at a higher level too early leads to a weak foundation, and worse, develop negative perceptions of not only the subject but of themselves as inept in Maths. I personally would rather spend more time reinforcing basics again and again before moving on. I wish teachers who draft teaching worksheets would realise that this craft is important; no matter how experienced a teacher is, every worksheet must be planned with careful thought. In designing

> *I strongly believe that more harm can be done to the morale of students, who feel that it is some deficiency within themselves that caused them to fail, when in reality, the subject matter was pitched (without diagnostic assessment) at a level beyond their cognitive readiness.*

the worksheets and even tests, the teacher must be highly aware of the concepts to be assessed. Nothing comes naturally.

I acknowledge that personally, I was far more successful with weak students than with students in the top classes. The reason is because it is much harder to pitch and pace for higher-ability students. The actual differences among high-ability students are much wider and disparate in this spectrum and one tends to raise the bar high. This leads to inevitable discouragement and frustration among good students. It is this phenomenon I see in this present day, particularly in the Integrated Programme (IP) curricula. The argument for teaching "A" Level material to Year Three or Four students with the intention to "stretch" their learning potential may sound challenging and innovative but for students who have difficulties, this is again, unduly demoralising. Having observed the curriculum designing process in various schools, I realise that standards are very often set arbitrarily. There was no evidence that the curriculum was pegged at the students' cognitive level corresponding to their age. My concern is that when the bar is set too high, the confidence and self-esteem of "normal" students will be inordinately affected, should they fail. Practically speaking, it is a more efficient use of time if a difficult concept is taught at the appropriate older age, when it can be grasped more easily. Teachers do need to reflect if the rush to teach more and more difficult material to younger and younger students is really benefitting them. I strongly believe that more harm can be done to the morale of students, who feel that it is some deficiency within themselves that caused them to fail, when in reality, the subject matter was pitched (without diagnostic assessment) at a level beyond their cognitive readiness.

Speaking of assessments and learning, I would like to offer my take on examinations at this point.

Education is a favourite topic for debate and discussion all over the world. Everyone has their two cents' worth of opinions because everyone is a by-product of an "education system". In the heat of debate, what most do not realise is, there are distinct differences in the terms that are often used, such as "education", "system", "school", "teaching" and "learning". These terms are not synonymous. Lots of resources may be poured into "programmes" in "education" for "outcome-based" purposes, but they may miss the mark for teaching and learning to take place. Measuring convoluted "education outcomes" with figures, statistics and rankings has little bearing on teaching and learning as well. These two elements, teaching and learning, stand apart from the system; they may or may not even *be* in a system!

I believe that examinations are needed as a means for cognitive engagement.

The most common reason for doing away with examinations is that these are unnecessarily stressful for the children. People who hold this view often fail to recognise the immensity of the role that examinations have in the development of the child. I believe that examinations are needed as a *means* for cognitive engagement. In preparing for an examination, students are exposed to very consequential thinking skills such as those required in inductive and deductive reasoning—critical thinking skills such as identifying, comparing, discriminating, assimilating, analysis, organising, synthesising. These are intricate and complex skills which form a "natural" set of skills needed to function effectively in the work environment. The students who are most able to master this skills set are the ones who are most ready for higher-order work. Besides, examinations also train the child's resilience, tenacity as well as other affective domains, which are much-needed qualities for personal and character development.

In my opinion, the removal of examinations at key points is therefore totally unwise. Teachers can attest to the great difference to learning when a child can bring his prior knowledge to the lesson as it will help him to be actively involved in the process. A key component needed for active learning is memory work. Without activating the use of the memory early in their learning journey, I believe that students may find themselves handicapped in the assimilation and application of concepts later at the higher levels. I strongly feel the lack of emphasis on memory work is impeding the progress of especially, the average student. Memory is an important component of the mind that can be trained and sharpened, which would then contribute to agility in thinking. There must be a balance between exploratory experiential learning and the active commitment to memory of essential facts that will build a foundation for whatever profession one chooses later in life.

As professionals, teachers should master the art and science of their craft to facilitate learning.

I am in favour of national examinations as it is an objective standard to measure if students have acquired the requisite knowledge, skills and techniques. Having said that, I detest a system that is overly focussed on examinations. Many times, the teaching of higher-order thinking and learning must be compromised because resources need to be devoted to delivering results. Therefore, my view is that the Primary School Leaving Examination (PSLE) is a necessary albeit blunt tool of assessment to guide students to the next phase of learning. Perhaps other assessments in the form of subjective observations of the students' curiosity, enquiry and participation should also be considered.

Finally, I think we can agree that there is no perfect system. I believe those who are concerned about the "system" and "exams" tend to rely on subjective observations and experience. I feel that in Singapore, the need for exams at certain levels outweighs its removal. As professionals, teachers should master the art and science of their craft to facilitate learning. Performance targets, rankings and the sheer volume of work sometimes distract teachers from honing their skills, but if they are committed to helping their students learn, they must reflect on their craft. How do they bring out the best in each child? How can they be more sensitive and perceptive when it comes to the invisible development of the mind? How can they elevate the thinking to a higher-order perspective?

My fourth experience arose from my having had the good fortune of working with a colleague, Ms W. K. Koh, in the Upper Secondary level in 1993. She had been one of the appointed Examiners for Additional Mathematics in the Sijil Peperiksaan Malaysia (SPM)

Examination, the equivalent of the GCE "O" Level examinations, offered by the Malaysian Examination Board. It was from her that I first learnt how Mathematics examination papers should be marked based on the criteria of accuracy, method and concepts—marking processes advised by the Cambridge Examiners. This approach was disseminated to local teachers some years after that by our MOE and it has always been a guide to marking examination papers since then. But I saw it as much more than that.

It was an eye-opener for me for I was never guided that way in marking papers. It was always a right or wrong mark before, but when I learnt the need to analyse the steps and make a judgment in deciding the awarding of marks, it shed a lot of light on my marking. I realised that this process should be considered not just merely at the point of marking examination and test papers; it should serve as a very important guide in the areas of our instruction when teaching, it should be our intended objectives for testing when we set exam questions as well as it should guide what we wish the outcome to be for the learners at the end of the assessment. I advocate every test and examination paper be thoroughly discussed by all the teachers teaching that level, when the marking scheme and alternative solutions as well as the anticipated mistakes should also be presented. Such meetings are critical to the

Assessments are too often seen as an outcome. Actually, it is a critical process where teaching and learning meet.

improvement of the teachers' concepts and pedagogies, ensuring a more balanced distribution of teacher quality within the level. Unfortunately, this process is often deemed to take up too much time or that teachers are unable to find a common time to meet and so it is not a common practice in schools. Assessments are too often seen as an outcome. Actually, it is a critical *process* where teaching and learning meet.

Teaching is easy; ensuring that learning takes place is difficult.

Along the way, I have also become acutely aware of the need to perceive whether learning and thinking has taken place when I teach. I rarely answer students' queries directly nor give them solutions to their difficulties. I search for the assimilation and integration of their knowledge or lack thereof, and by continually asking them questions, help them to search for the understanding within themselves and their repertoire of knowledge. This will help students to learn and see how to apply themselves. Very often, it is their lack of careful reading of the questions which caused them to miss key information. Their lack of analysis or reluctance to go beyond surface reading is a barrier that must be broken through to reach higher-order thinking.

Teaching is easy; ensuring that learning takes place is difficult. To do so, to seek conceptual understanding and to have the understanding of cognitive engagement and learner awareness are indispensable considerations that teachers must be fully aware of, in order to attain mastery in teaching.

Two men looked out from prison bars; one saw the mud, the other saw stars.

Frederick Langbridge

CHAPTER 4
AFFECTIVE DEVELOPMENT

In life, we often see things in a binary fashion. In reality, one never sees entirely nothing but mud, nor another see entirely nothing but stars. Life is a spectrum that spans the lowest of darkness to the epitome of brightness.

As teachers, we enter the lives of our young people and how we guide them to reach nearer the stars can make a huge difference in their lives. Many of us enter teaching with noble ideals. We consciously try to inculcate values, promote character development and act as good role models, in the hope that such "seeds" implanted in our students' hearts and minds will take root, grow and blossom in time. Yet, very often, it is the subconscious, kind gestures and words which can have a profound and lasting impact, touching an inner chord.

Let me share a personal encounter with an individual whose words remain a permanent affirmation of my worth.

In May 1982, I received news that I had failed my second year in University. In those days, if you failed the supplementary examination of a module, you repeated the whole year, including all the modules you had passed. It was a very bitter experience, especially when I had not known failure of such a nature in my life. My teaching bursary was suspended and honestly, my life was in disarray then. In moments of escapism, I even considered discontinuing my studies. Frankly, I never did like to be tied down by academics and a rigid system, which was how I felt about my University course then.

Due to my involvement with co-curricular activities at the University, I had the opportunity to become acquainted with a University personnel who was sympathetic and suggested that I explore the option of applying for a post in a research company. I took up the recommendation, not realising that the firm would carry out the interviews in the most professional manner. I was not prepared for it, nor was I sure what was happening throughout the three to four hours during which I was put through a battery of tests. I just remembered many passages to analyse, many questions to answer, and it seemed endless. I was fatigued at the end of it all.

> ***I decided to never ever under-value myself on the basis of grades of any kind. Nor ever allow this to colour my perception of my students.***

It was late afternoon when I was finally called for a face-to-face interview with a senior executive in the company, an expatriate. He asked about my background and I was forthcoming in sharing with him my dilemma of whether to continue my university studies or to drop out and find a job. He listened intently and advised me to consider carefully. He very kindly analysed my state of mind and laid out the options before me. I had a bond to pay off if I were to leave the University in this manner. Frankly, it seemed so obvious that I was being childish and impetuous. I was embarrassed that he was spending this amount of time with me.

What stunned me however, was his finishing statement which I will never forget. He ended with, "However, should you really wish to leave the University, I will offer you the post of a junior executive in my company. The university's loss will be our gain."

I could not believe my ears. There I was, a failure, rejected by the prestigious National University of Singapore; yet, here he was, a person with his feet planted firmly on the commercial ground, who could see my worth beyond that of a University education, based on an evaluation of results from the tests I had taken! Such affirmation from a total stranger, who could perceive value unlike the way society measured it! I must be one of the most fortunate persons in the world to have had this profound validation. It made a permanent impression on me, and I decided to never ever under-value myself on the basis of grades of any kind. Nor ever allow this to colour my perception of my students.

As teachers, we receive letters of thanks and appreciation, all of which are received with much joy—not that we look to receiving a reward, but every expression of thanksgiving does help to encourage us.

In a similar fashion, what is it that we teachers can do to encourage the affective development of our kids? The impact for some may be momentary while for others, it could affect them profoundly, for life. We may need to be reminded that in the way we carry ourselves, we are role models. In our observations of the interests and aptitudes of our students, we can point them toward particular career paths. By believing in them and helping them attain an aspiration they thought was a lost cause, we can help them surpass what they may not have believed possible.

It is hard for this present generation to imagine what life was like in the 1980s; even a school of some renown did not have many school facilities. Not every household had a fixed telephone line and resources were very much fewer than today. To be fair, the Ministry of Education did what it could to provide information about the avenues available to students beyond school then, but I feel that these were often not effectively disseminated.

Recently, I was reconnected with a student from 1989 and though I had forgotten the details, I was glad to read of what she had recalled that had determined her career pathway then.

> *"It has been nearly 3 decades since Miss Sie taught me. The thing about her that I hold dear is the fact that she is a teacher who truly cares about her students. She cares not just about their academic performance but also their well-being, and most importantly, their future. She is nurturing and encouraging. She told us that we could be more. She stood by us while others lost faith. She believed in us.*

Art was my favourite subject in school. At a tender age, I knew I wanted to pursue a career which was art-related. I did not know what kind of a job it would be. I only knew that I never wanted to stop studying art.

I took Art as a subject at 'O' Levels. During my time, there were only 2 classes in Crescent Girls' School who did art. I wanted to be in the Arts stream, as that was the only stream offering Art as a subject. One could argue that there was the option of taking art classes outside of school. But it was not a viable option for me because my parents were only able to meet our basic needs like shelter, food, and education. Anything else was frivolous. So the only way to continue pursuing art was to take it as a subject in school. The 11th class of my school did History and Art as part of their syllabus, while the 12th (last) class studied Geography and Art. And that was the combination I picked, not knowing that I would be placed in the last class.

Being in the last class of my cohort caused my morale to dip. Many people (teachers included) judged my class. They thought that we were academically weak and lacked the motivation to excel. And that 'you study Art because you are not good at your studies.' I resented that assumption with much contempt—I still do. When you are 16 with raging hormones, anything negative is magnified a million times and I plunged into a pit of self-doubt and insecurity. This mental state of mind is not good for a student who will be taking a major exam at the end of the year. I remember having to constantly remind myself that I could prove the critics wrong by getting good grades. I studied like my life depended on it, and having a caring form teacher was such a great comfort. Miss Sie made us feel that she'd got our backs. And I knew that with a dedicated Maths teacher like her, scoring a distinction for this subject was achievable.

I recall vividly the time Miss Sie brought the class to Baharuddin Vocational Institute (their students were very strong in Graphic Design) and Nanyang Academy of Fine Arts. She did not have to do this, but she did. She exposed us to possibilities and showed that there was a future for Art students. My parents were not well-informed. It helped me tremendously to know what my choices were and Miss Sie was my only gateway. I remember feeling very grateful for what she did to open our eyes. In 1989, when there was no internet, it was a challenge to go out there to find information, and at 16, I really did not know where to look. On top of that, there was no one in my family and social circle who studied Art. I was a frog in the well, not knowing the paths which were out there.

I wished to go to a junior college after 'O' Levels. Tuition fees at NAFA were beyond my parents' means. The turning point came when Miss Sie handed me a form for admission to the Art Elective Programme (AEP). I had never heard of that, and suddenly, I saw light at the end of the tunnel. I now had a goal and I was going to work towards it! At that time, only National Junior College (NJC) and Nanyang Junior College (NYJC) offered

AEP at 'A' Levels. I had my heart set at NJC. The curriculum for the AEP was all rounded. Students who made it were exposed to many forms of art, not just drawing and painting, but photography, design, print-making, pottery, art history, etc. It would be a dream come true if I could make it there!

With a clear goal in mind, studying hard to reach it was a no-brainer. And with Miss Sie, the Great Motivator, I did well for my Prelims and 'O' Levels and made it! That was a great confidence booster. People think highly of students from NJC, and wait, you are in the Art Elective Programme too? 'Wow, you are not only smart but artistic and talented too!' (insert eye-roll)

However, I still say, the most important characteristic of a teacher is the way one carries oneself in the course of duty. Perhaps my constant belief in abiding by "Simple in Virtue, Steadfast in Duty" in all my duties towards my students has been my greatest strength.

It was also in the AEP that I discovered graphic design. It dawned on me that this was what I really wanted to pursue in the long run. After my 'A' Levels, I did graphic design at Temasek Polytechnic School of Design (converted from Baharuddin Vocational Institute). I have been in this line for two decades now. I feel like I have never worked a single day because I am doing what I truly love. There are no words to describe how thankful I am to know this rare and special teacher."

Koh Soo Peng, Class of 1989, CGS. Written in 2018.

I have always been a believer of Career Guidance, knowing how much a child can be motivated if he can find his direction. In later years, when resources were far more readily available, the students became more aware of the many options they had. However, during the 1980s and early 1990s, this was definitely not the case. In her case, I am glad that Soo Peng has come such a long way with just a little help. Like how Miss Daisy Wee had valued me, I had helped to make a child feel valued as well.

"I feel I have to take this chance to say 'thank you' for all you've done for me. As you know, I'm not a very good talker but if there's one thing I'm confident about, that is writing. In all my years in Primary school and Secondary school, I believe you're the only teacher that have actually 'seen' me for what I am and not as a shadow with a name. I was quite shocked that you took the trouble to 'notice' and 'know' me, and even more shocked that you should like my writing.

[...] Miss Sie, it was you that helped me regain my long-lost confidence and really opened another door for me, a door

of light and a faint hope that I never expected to come from anyone. You can't imagine my joy when you asked me to submit an entry for the Commonwealth Essay Competition! I was amazed, bewildered, delighted... all three at the same time! You can't imagine how grateful I felt! I guess, Miss Sie, you are so approachable, encouraging, and most importantly, a willing listener, that I feel no qualms telling you my inner-most thoughts. Thank you, Miss Sie, for being a wonderful teacher. As I said, I'm never going to look back."

Tan Yi-Ling, 1994 cohort in SCGS. Written in 1994.

Yi-Ling is of course, in an element of her own, and she soon found her niche through scholarships and is now an established educator in her own right.

I am definitely not one of those whom one would consider a charismatic type of teacher. I have a good sense of humour, but above all, I am exacting, have high expectations that I set for myself first, before I expect them of my students. I have a temper and can be quite sharp in correcting students, but never unkindly. One of my innate strengths is strong observation and analysis and this has helped me, perhaps intuitively, guide students to overcome their difficulties. However, I still say, the most important characteristic of a teacher is the way one carries oneself in the course of duty. Perhaps my constant belief in abiding by "Simple in Virtue, Steadfast in Duty" in all my duties towards my students has been my greatest strength.

In the next section, I share some of my correspondences with my students, to illustrate more clearly how the impact of a teacher can take a direction which we least expect.

"My Additional Maths teacher has started a foundation in me, not just in Math, but also in terms of my character and personality. Her devotion and hard work touched me deeply, and I am determined to work hard, and become a brand new 'Cynthia'. No one would have guessed that the change in me is mostly due to this respected teacher of mine. Because of her, my attitude towards Maths, school and myself has changed.

[...] Sometimes, I wonder why this teacher did not try to become a psychologist. Why do I say this? Simply because she can judge our personality and character, almost 100% right. Whenever we were depressed or happy, she would be able to tell. I remember an incident when I got so frustrated not being able to do 'Logarithm', I even created my 'own rules' and did my work my own way. When this teacher saw it during a Saturday remedial lesson, she got quite frustrated and told me that I was one person who always created my 'own rules' and did my things my own way. I was rather affected by what my teacher said, and was determined to practise on my own at home. My teacher noticed that I was able to answer her questions in class and knew that I revised my work at home during the weekend. As a result of her slight scolding, I got 37/40 for my Logarithm

test. So far, I have not failed any Maths test, and this is a major change."

Cynthia, 1999 cohort in SCGS. Written in 1999, in an essay entitled "The teacher who caused a turning point in my life".

The change in this child in her learning of Maths was marked. I distinctly remember that remedial lesson. It was almost futile because she was fixated on what she felt was "right" in the application of the laws of logarithm despite the many examples shown to her. She was blocking her own learning. I did remember the difference that took place after the weekend when I checked on her by way of my "graded" exercise technique and was pleasantly surprised that she had broken through the barrier. Thereafter, she blazed her own way. I only realised the impact I had on her towards the end of Secondary Four, some 18 months later. And it was gratifying.

In an earlier chapter, I had mentioned the impact that I had felt from a question, "When teachers gave remediation lessons, are they remedying their teaching or their students' learning?" I took this to heart. I know teachers supporting students in a remediation programme are vital, especially in the areas of academic weakness. But teachers must first do much self-reflection as well as preparation to attain maximum good.

I took great pains thereafter to improve in every aspect of my teaching, be it pedagogical, like the use of various instructional strategies, or the use of IT to enhance learning. Most importantly, I always ensured a very clear delivery, avoiding superfluity of words, being always precise and punctual, and checking that, as far as possible, no child was lost. Again, my strategy of the "graded" exercise to monitor my students closely always helped me to track students effectively.

One may say, it is only an hour's worth of time. But if 20 students were to attend, the time lost is 20 hours. Remediation should be such that the students would gain more by being with you for that one hour than if they had struggled on their own.

In later years, when I mentored younger teachers, I always reminded them that remedial lessons should always be similarly prepared well. If a remedial lesson is an hour, and there is only an attempt at producing a worksheet which is prepared without much thought, it is not good enough. One may say, it is only an hour's worth of time. But if 20 students were to attend, the time lost is 20 hours. Remediation should be such that the students would gain more by being with you for that one hour than if they had struggled on their own. This is especially so for revision lessons. It is pointless if the teacher is merely regurgitating facts which the students could have revised on their own. But if the lessons are structured such that it would enhance their recollection, establish connections in their learning and help them reach a higher plane, then the ideal standard of remediation is attained.

Whilst I had embarked on my research pathway in 2012, I also gave myself to adjunct teaching in a neighbourhood school. Whichever school I was teaching in made no difference to the amount of time I would spend with the kids. I was pleasantly surprised and immeasurably touched to receive the message below some six years later from a quiet student who wrote when he learnt about my illness. I deeply appreciate his observations and reception of the work I had rendered with my heart.

"You kept track of each student's weaknesses, spent more time than any other teacher on Saturdays to drill us, give us practice papers, test after test, in order to make sure we got the concepts right. I am very thankful for your patience and effort that you put into the class. It wasn't easy, especially when time was limited and you did everything you could to make sure we did well.

However, I failed you back then. I did not attain the 'A' grade that you were expecting, but only achieved B3 for E Maths and B4 for A Maths. Nevertheless, I am very glad that you were the one that taught me, it would have been very different if I had any other teacher for Math.

I want to let you know that you have made an impact on my life; you are the best teacher I've ever had and the one I respect the most. I admire your passion for teaching. It's truly amazing and it made a huge difference in many peoples' lives."

Yap Guan Sheng, 2012 cohort in JWSS. Written in 2018.

It seems inevitable that we always measure ourselves by the results we receive and that it is by results that we "repay" teachers for their efforts. This boy went on to do well in the Polytechnic and is now embarking on his Computer Science course at NTU. I am very gratified to see him pressing ahead so positively.

The 1997 cohort was a weak batch in the school I was teaching in and there were many students who needed "rescuing" after the preliminary examinations. That was a year I did not have Additional Maths classes and I was roped in to help with remediating small groups. Good progress was made although I do remember I was unable to help one of the students. What I totally did not expect was that 20 years later, I was to receive words of acknowledgement from this chance teaching encounter that had had a far more profound impact than I had realised.

I was immensely surprised one day to find a note in my messenger box on Facebook from a girl that I had to take time to recall. I vaguely remembered a very quiet, docile girl, who might not have been regular for those remedial sessions, but had been co-operative whenever she attended.

> *"I was quite the terrible student back then, but you had very kindly, and surprisingly (to me), asked me to come along to the revision classes. I'm not sure why at that point in time, I didn't think many teachers outside of my own form class teacher would have given me a second thought, but you had, and for that I will always be grateful. I loathe to sound cliché or dramatic, but your gesture was the turning point in my*

life. I have been living overseas since 2001 but throughout this time, I have been periodically looking for a way to get in touch with you. Thank God for Facebook! I'm really glad to have found your profile, as I would really love to have the opportunity to formally and properly say a very heartfelt 'thank you so much'."

Sabrina, 1997 cohort in SCGS. Written in 2017.

We did meet up a couple of months back and had a wonderful time. I learnt how much this girl had gone through in her teenage years to overcome the various obstacles in her learning journey, and perhaps I had just entered her life at a pivotal point. That she has gone on to obtain her doctorate in Psychology and could identify that this had been an event that had marked her life just as the expatriate in that research company had marked mine, is really paying it forward in life.

With her was a more exuberant classmate whose turnaround in her results was quite dramatic. Here, she articulates how the sessions had helped her in her learning pathway at that time.

"Both Sabrina and I were extremely lucky as we were selected and handpicked from the powers that be to attend your remedial lessons for A & E maths. Yes I know it was a long time ago but it has left such an indelible mark on both our lives! Indeed, it was my 'aha' light bulb moment. You turned me from an 'F9' (during preliminary exams) to an 'A1' for my 'O' levels. I always

thought, knew and believed strongly that I was not a maths person and would never have the aptitude for it. But the proof is in the pudding and we were triumphant when our maths results surpassed everyone's expectations! We had tasted sweet victory and you were instrumental in our learning process.

But more importantly, the internal transformation and spiritual footprint you left in our lives is even more enduring. I actually started to see myself through your lens, that I can study and I can do this. That self-belief helped me tremendously through my adulthood and I realised that it has EVERYTHING to do with who was teaching and how they teach. You Rock Teaching. You Teach with a capital T with no ifs or buts. Simple and elegant—you just knew how to teach.

[...] You never taught us before and was given the mammoth and dubious task of transforming our academic results. I thought we needed a miracle. And boy did we receive one when you worked your magic changing us from 'inside out'. As opposed to the top down 'outside in' method where the voice of authority dictates our behaviour for a hopefully more favourable outcome.

You did not judge us nor focus on our issues or problems. When we were 16 years old, we had the weight of the world on our shoulders with so many insecurities. I had to put on a rebellious, brave front to get through it all. But you were not bothered with labels like 'naughty', 'hopeless', 'ill-disciplined kids'. Instead, you taught us from a place of respect, compassion and kindness. To be treated as an equal was the 'magic wand' we needed. That afternoon, you shared a particular memory in uni which made you feel like an underdog. And that was when I realised why you got us. Because you had been there before and knew exactly how we felt about ourselves."

Greta, 1997 cohort in SCGS. Written in 2018.

At this juncture, the point I wish to make is, as teachers we do need to make a distinction and decide when to "ignore" problems and focus totally on engaging the cognitive mind. In fact, I do make it a point never to focus on a student's emotional issues, be it personal, family or relationship matters. Our focus in the classroom should be a cognitive engagement and when we can entice the student's mind to learn, it inadvertently does help to sort out many other emotions. Talking about "problems" is often circular. The truth is, many problems in life have no solutions and more often than not, time is what is needed to sort them out.

... when we can entice the student's mind to learn, it inadvertently does help to sort out many other emotions. Talking about "problems" is often circular.

It is more important for teachers to diagnose the cognitive interference, help the child to concentrate and use different strategies to attain the desired outcome. There is never a foolproof method so observation and objectivity must be applied. It goes without saying that the teacher should have full competency in concept mastery of subject matter, a full repertoire of teaching strategies and loads of patience. The only time I found I could not help to achieve the desired state was due to the lack of time leading up to the examinations. Sadly, in a couple of cases, it was also due to a lack of will on the students' part. These were, however, rare circumstances.

Cognitive and affective development go hand in hand, and there are times that one would be given more focus than the other. I strongly believe that cognitive development is a science and art that has not been well understood and applied in our teaching arena. I have come to this conclusion intuitively through my pathway as a teacher and would have wished to have been able to learn and document more about this important tenet in teaching.

On a less serious note, the students whom I came across in the Specialised IP schools were of a different nature. Here, relationships between teachers and students are far more akin to a mentoring one for the period together is longer than the duration of being a "form" teacher to a class. How one student "clicks" with a teacher is often not quite explicable. Having taught Ryan in 2008–2009, I was surprised when he kept in touch with me through the subsequent years, and below, I include a short extract of some of our conversations when he was pondering his life choices concerning his University course. In many ways, I love the way that teaching can grow into mentoring of this nature and it is a form of self-actualisation for myself as well.

11 June 2013

Hi Ms Sie, How are you? as you can see from the time and desperation of my message, I am still incredibly disturbed on something and its regarding my choice for university again. If its convenient, I would be glad to have your take on this matter. During the first year of NS, I have accepted SUTD's bond-free scholarship before deciding to ditch it and to accept NUS Industrial & Systems engineering course. Though I feel at home with SUTD's style, I went with my mother's advice to stick with NUS because its safer. Of course, many issues come to mind, such as credibility, job security, learning experience and all. Until this day I am still torn over my choice, but recently I have managed to snag a corporate scholarship (bond of 4 years) which erases my problem of job security (none of these would have happened if not for my entry to NUS High School). CEO of the corporation happened to be on the board of trustees in SUTD and he saw that I had rejected SUTD's scholarship. He advised me that it might be worth it to try out the new education reason being that the government is spending so much on it. I do feel inclined to switch back to SUTD, one of the main reasons being that I would probably do (much, much, i believe) better in a hands on environment, rather than just books (NUS). A reason holding back would be the quality of students that the SUTD has accepted (at least when compared to NUS industrial system engine, mostly straight As). Would the creativity of SUTD outweigh the credibility of NUS, or would this idealistic approach of SUTD soon be brought down to reality like the NUS High School system? One of the biggest advantages of NUS High over JCs, at least to me, is the opportunities for research, and this opportunities might have allowed many students to find more passion, which i find important for fuelling further studies and SUTD has almost the same X-factor (research opportunities). I have recently met up with A to find out how was freshmen year in SUTD like for him. It was very challenging and he said not many people cope well, but at the same time through his complaints I could tell that he is enjoying his time there. When I asked him if he believes that he has made the right choice, he answered that THAT question is on everyone's (including his cohort's) mind and he has no answer for it yet. I do remember you being a supporter for SUTD the last time we spoke, and I do hope to hear your inputs. I know I kind of sound like I have already made up my mind but I value your views highly. Worth it to "risk" it all over again? On a side note it would be much easier to hold a GPA of 4.0 (usual scholarship requirements) in SUTD compared to NUS. O and I am really, really glad that things turned out to be better on your side.

11 June 2013

Hi Ryan, I see 3 points in what you have written.

1) the process of decision making

2) NUS vs SUTD

3) personal factors wrt (1) and (2)

1) *Decision Making*

There are decisions that affect life and death and there is no turning back. this includes war/crisis/health risks like to take or not to take an operation. in such cases, there is no right or wrong decision. It's just the stakes are high, and whatever the outcome, one needs courage to bear.

There are decisions that do affect morals and principles, hence there can be a right or wrong decision. And the wrong decision is costly.

There are decisions that one makes in good faith, but may or may not turn out well and one has to work at it to move ahead. Most serious of these should be marriage. Sometimes decision to migrate. Making a total switch of career midway etc.

There are decisions that is a pros and cons choice. Many decisions in life fall in this category. What is important in such cases is, whatever decision one makes, dont regret, don't look back. Nothing is lost, nothing is irrecoverable. Perhaps maybe in terms of opportunities. But, then, what is yours is yours. Opportunities is always a chance factor.

In this last category, weighing the pros and cons, seeking different views are sound moves, which you have done. Because you are young, and this is a major decision, hence you are "troubled". But it is a happy "trouble" because you have choices, and good choices where many do not have. So it is a happy trouble. ☺

2) *NUS vs SUTD*
It is not fair to compare a new institution with and established institution. Then people always do.

I support SUTD because I saw the initial presentation and believe they have done proper homework and has a strong entrepreneurial approach, with creativity. It is unfortunate about the calibre of people that they take. I heard about this from other sources. But the reason is because many strong students rejected them going for the most established route. In a way, it is like "success begets success". So they are at a disadvantage, but I hope that will not be for long.

The pros of SUTD you already have seen. Complaints are inevitable whichever institute you go in, as there will never be a total win-win situation. But, because it is in the initial years, I think, there will be alot of opportunities and they will do their best to make it work. If A can't say whether his decision is "right", that's not bad because he is very critical. So being neutral is really positive for him. I have met B and C and I remembered they were happy.

For reputation, NUS wins hands down. For an adventurous exploration, you know the answer.

btw, in my personal opinion, NUS High is still the school with the best direction among the IP schools. My only worry, is the lack of seriousness and rigour that students may have problem when they meet a totally exam system.

3) *Personal Factors*
Since you have secured a scholarship and hence a job (Congratulations!!!!), there is no worry in this direction. Frankly, I dont believe that it would be a worry at all. If you are good, from any unis, it does not make a difference. People blame external factors, instead of taking a good look at themselves and their attitude.

In the end, why you already have your inclination is because of that free spirit in yourself. You know the answer. Your heart tells you. Your mind tells you that the pros and cons weigh up. But it is a plunge. You are in NDU. You know it takes guts to plunge.

I think you know the answer.
And whatever your choice, just hold on, and push ahead. There is no right or wrong decision. Beat out the path for yourself in your decision.

And whether NUS or SUTD, I will support your decision. 🙂

And yes, honestly, I remain a supporter of SUTD, just as I remain a supporter of NUS High, without which, I will never have met the most interesting kids. 😀

14 Sept 2015

Hi Ms Sie, Hope you are still doing well. Been wanting to write to you since the beginning of the year but I guess I just got swept along by the distractions of life. Today marks the first day of my second year in this university and thus far I have nothing but praises for it. Apart from the watered down MIT education that we are receiving, it is very much about the people that I interact with every day as well. Seems like everybody is subconsciously or consciously looking for something different in their higher education as compared to their peers. People here might not be the smartest but a great amount of them are very passionate in what they love. Recently I am back from a 10-week exchange program in MIT. I loved how they added ceramics, drawing and critical writing classes in our coursework. In fact, our main course was on building an electric boat with virtually any way we want with a high budget. It was mad to think that students with only 1 year of basic university education could complete such a crazy project. But we did it and almost all our boats managed to travel in the water, in fact far surpassing the performance of the instructor boats. Highlights of the exchange program of course include being able to take road trips to nearby places such as Montreal and New York City. It was the kind of trip that I could not pinpoint what changed in me until I got back to Singapore, and I realized I do not look at things the same way again. "To my mind, the greatest reward and luxury of travel is to be able to experience everyday things as if for the first time, to be in a position in which almost nothing is so familiar it is taken for granted."— Bill Bryson. Lastly, I would like to share a small segment of lyrics from the song "A letter to me" by Brad Paisley (it is a soulful song if you haven't heard it yet): "And you should really thank Mrs. Brinkman. She spends so much extra time. It's like she sees the diamond underneath. And she's polishing you 'til you shine." Thank you for making a difference in my life. Happy belated teacher's day, Ryan Tse

18 Sept 2015

It's always a pleasure to hear from you, to know how you are getting on, to listen to your thoughts as you journey on—to me, this is more vivid than looking at photographs taken, for these are reflections of the mind and soul. I consider it my privilege to have a glimpse of your life and rejoice to see your growth and purposefulness, the enlargement of your mind and vision as you venture out of the boundaries of mere classroom. I have never heard the song, and did look it up on YouTube. Yes, it is a soulful country song. Thank you for remembering me in the lyrics. I am touched. Very. Wishing the best for you as you continue the exploration of the intellect and creativity, and in the reapings, do remember those lesser than you. Always. That's true education and humanity. SSH

23 Aug 2016

Hi Miss Sie,
Hope you are doing well. Yesterday during a road trip in western Norway, we picked up this Singaporean old lady who rode with us for about half an hour. She was a teacher her whole life but has spent majority of her time travelling the world, while living partially in Norway. She was telling us things like "take calculated risks, see the world but don't tell your parents," etc stuff that reminds me of you. Attached is her blog. (although I doubt you're the kind to publicly blog about anything)

Ryan

27 July 2017

Hi Ms Sie, how are you! Time flies, I remember consulting you for my college decision, and yet in 3 weeks I am going to graduate and head off to the world. Recently I've been giving thanks to a humanities professor for introducing an impactful book that I really liked, and he told me that the gratitude he gets makes his profession as an educator fulfilling, hence that really reminded me of you. Ryan

27 July 2017

Congratulations 😀
By the grace and mercies of God, I have been preserved thus far. Presently relief teaching at NUS HS this semester.

Thanks for remembering me. It's always lovely to hear from you. As you grow through the years, may you be granted the wisdom to impact and inspire yet another generation to live fulfilling lives.

All the best to all your future endeavours! 🙂

Email exchanges with Ryan, 2008 cohort in NUS HS.

Written between 2013–2017.

We all know as teachers we can impact students in a positive or a negative way. Most of the time, we would share things that have gone well. But there were many instances when it did not. I have always felt that I made mistakes at the expense of other children and there must be some that I had inadvertently hurt. It is through many years of introspection that I have realised how much my own upbringing, including the television programmes and movies of that era, had influenced me.

Coming from a dialect-speaking background, I grew up in a very Chinese environment although this was counter-balanced at school. I am not sure whether this is Eastern or Western, but it seemed that when we perceived a negative influence, we had the habit of making judgment and "warning" students to stay away from that person. In fact, in the earlier days, it was not uncommon to believe that by shouting at a student to "wake up" the student, the message somehow would get through, and the message could be shouted into his mind. Television shows and movies also often depicted this. But on what basis did we decide that someone was a negative influence? And based on whose judgement? That is the question. Even so, is that idea to keep away really a right way of teaching? An incident that stood out for me in 1993 taught me a lesson I will never forget.

One afternoon, a student looked me up in school and asked me directly to my face, "What is it that you feel is not right about me?" I was taken aback. I asked her for clarification. She said, "You told D that I am not a good influence, that she should keep away from me." I was speechless. I could not even remember the context in which I had allegedly said those words, though I had to acknowledge that I had felt that she was not a compliant student and that she was under some negative influence outside of school. I could not put my finger on it. What she subsequently said, hit home hard. She said, "I always respected you. Had you thought there was a problem with me, you could have told me." I knew at that moment. I had no answer but only to apologise, that I had been wrong and biased. How easily as teachers we arrive at a conclusion with what we perceive to be valid observations! Yet how often, we could be wrong.

For, just as an impactful word can inspire one for a lifetime, likewise a damaging word leaves an indelible scar.

Learning is therefore continual. It is easy to think we have arrived, that we should be put on a pedestal, only to find we could be falling back into the ways in which we find we are lacking. More than 20 years later, a 16-year-old boy asked to have a short talk with me. He was not exactly an attentive student in class due to his varied interests and a hyper-active mind. I had noted that he seemed to have a strong fear of his father and I had "used" it a few times to manipulate him into co-operating better in class. That did not go down well with him and he chose to talk it over with me, saying that I could have tried to appeal to his sense of reason rather than use such a strategy. I accepted his point and appreciated his forthrightness.

I hope I have caused less hurt and done more good in my years of teaching. For, just as an impactful word can inspire one for a lifetime, likewise a damaging word leaves an indelible scar.

PART 2

Defining the Race Course

*Two roads diverged
in a wood, and I—
I took the one less
travelled by,
and that has made
all the difference.*

Robert Frost

CHAPTER 5
THE ROAD LESS TRAVELLED—MY TEACHING PATHWAY

"The key to wisdom in these circumstances is to make the distinction between discrete good and systemic good. When you are in the grip of a big, complex mess, you have the power to do discrete good but probably not systemic good."

David Brooks on The Planning Fallacy[1]

I remember being struck by these words when I first read it in an article some time ago. However complex the mess, one can do what one can within the circumference of one's situation. The issue is not how big the circumference is. Having worked in many schools, I have seen teachers who see teaching as a job or a career. However, I also see many teachers who see teaching as a calling and vocation. Their hearts are warmer as they truly want to mould lives

[1] *Brooks, 2011*

and nurture children. Seeing these dedicated and principled teachers encouraged me to keep going. I was not alone. The present education system may be messy, but we are able to, and should, continue to do discrete good.

My experience in teaching is somewhat unique in that I entered the education system when the education landscape was evolving to explore outside of the existing system. Whilst one may criticise it as a mere change in form, in actual fact, there were many good and positive changes that had definitely benefitted many students.

When these changes began with selected schools being granted independent status in 1989, I joined one of them from 1991 to 2000. I was always acutely aware of Singapore's education pathway from the 1970s, having chosen to read the history of Singapore education as a module in my Diploma in Education days. I always wanted to be among the educators who could make changes for the better in the education of the children.

I had the good fortune of staying on in that independent school with an excellent principal for ten years. At that time, every student faced the GCE "O" level examinations, so students worked consistently over the secondary school years to cross this high-stakes examination. In this school, teachers had the liberty to teach in a variety of ways as well as introduce programmes. It was never a "drill and drill" process where students just memorised and regurgitated the "right" answers. In other words, being in a system with a national examination did not constrain our programme.

The Principal had clear educational values, and this was clearly translated in action. Similarly, the Vice-Principal was magnanimous in her support for her teachers and constantly encouraged innovation, giving us space to explore and be creative in our ideas. In those ten years, I took my students to sit in a court case and visit the Parliament House for English lessons. When it was time for debate lessons, every student in the class debated, not just the best speakers. And in Maths, we had games, projects, and competition training, all for the fun of learning and not for results.

When it was time for debate lessons, every student in the class debated, not just the best speakers. And in Maths, we had games, projects, and competition training, all for the fun of learning and not for results.

Many of the journal tasks I designed as alternative assessments at a specialised Math school eight years later were initiated in those days, where many ideas were at the inchoate stage. I either had little time to carry them out, or was only able to do so on a much smaller scale. Non-academic exposure was prioritised via various programmes—there was a work experience programme and job shadowing, which included visits to hotels to see how the culinary section operated—all simple initiatives that involved little cost.

I was very lucky to have the space and freedom to initiate these programmes and learn more about how the students learn. There was no work review then and the pay scale followed a fixed structure with no performance bonus to speak of. We did not even dream of using these means to chalk up personal points for our career advancement.

We did it because we loved our kids. That was enough motivation in itself. We derived great joy from teaching when we saw the students' eyes light up, conveying that "click" of understanding as concepts fell into place in their minds. We experienced jubilation when the students overcame their personal learning obstacles.

I owe much to the Principal and Vice-Principal of the school, whose vision, foresight and trust in their teachers gave us such liberty to plan, innovate and allow us to fulfil our education ideals to educate students. It was never for achievement in exams.

And we did very well for the national exams just by purely focussing on conceptual teaching, not "drilling" and forcing memorisation. I remember clearly my Principal saying that it was "beneath us" to chase after ranking numbers. What a leader! I was really very fortunate to have worked under her.

This period was a critical period of my teaching life. I owe much to the Principal and Vice-Principal of the school, whose vision, foresight and trust in their teachers gave us such liberty to plan, innovate and allow us to fulfil our education ideals to educate students. It was never for achievement in exams. Without these ten years of teaching and learning, I would be a very different teacher.

Towards the end of my stint in that school, then Prime Minister, Mr Goh Chok Tong, launched the new vision of "Thinking Schools, Learning Nation". This signalled the transition from an era of an "efficiency-driven" system to an "ability-driven" system to meet the challenges in the nation's future. To support this vision, the Ministry of Education allowed schools greater autonomy to tailor programmes to suit the characteristics of learners in their institutions, as well as to develop the niche strengths of each institute.[2]

From this springboard, the Integrated Programme (IP) was introduced in 2004, a programme allowing the top-performing students of the Primary School Leaving Examinations (PSLE) to do a direct six-year programme, without having to sit for the GCE "O" Level examinations. The IP takes in the top 10% of the cohort of the year whilst students enrolled in the Gifted Education Programme (GEP) are identified as the top 1% of their cohort.[3] Indeed, what constitutes the IP is likely to vary amongst the institutes that gained official approval from the Ministry of Education to run the programme. The educational pathways of these IP students culminate in either the GCE "A" Levels examinations or a diploma. The introduction of IP was intended to empower schools and teachers to be novel in their pedagogical reforms without compromising academic outcomes,[4] therefore providing schools with greater opportunities to innovate curriculum. This was both an exciting and innovative move that can be perceived as a reflection of the growing confidence in teacher expertise, as well as professionalism in the ownership and leadership of curriculum development in the schools. I remembered reading the ongoing discussion whilst not in any teaching institution

[2] *Gopinathan & Deng, 2006; Ng, 2008* [3] *Kang, 2004* [4] *Koh et. al., 2014, p. 853*

at that time. Today, the type of programme each school offers, and the structure in the organization of the six-year programme vary considerably. There are six distinct models, with variations within each model. (See Appendix)

> ***I particularly agree with the emphasis on encouraging students to engage in service... wherein they learn to respect the rights and dignity of the people around them.***

After a short hiatus, I began a new phase of learning and teaching when I re-entered the teaching service in 2003 as a flexi-adjunct teacher. I will always be grateful to the then Minister of Education, Mr Tharman Shanmugaratnam, for this opportunity. He actively showed he valued experienced teachers and created the avenues for us to return to the teaching service.

In 2007, I taught in a six-year IP school culminating in the International Baccalaureate (IB) programme. Founded in Geneva in 1968, it aimed to create an education structure which was academically rigorous and universally accepted, yet innovative in its methods for building a deep understanding of how their studies fit into the wider context of the world. Alongside academic studies, students are involved in a range of activities that encourage creativity, physical activity and service. I particularly agree with the emphasis on encouraging students to engage in service; i.e. providing unpaid, voluntary services wherein they learn to respect

"Vision Into the Next Century"—An exhibition put up as part of SCGS' centenary celebrations in 1999, where a "Liberalised Curriculum" was proposed and later became reality.

the rights and dignity of the people around them. With fifty years behind it, the International Baccalaureate Organisation has had the benefit of time to continually tweak and improve its curriculum and methods to develop truly independent learners. I was, and still am, very much impressed by the IB programme: its conceptualisation, its vision and its execution.

When I subsequently received the offer to teach in a specialised school with its own six-year diploma programme, my pathway diverged from the established IB path. It was in many ways, the pinnacle of my teaching career. To be able to have a role in designing a curriculum at a whole-school level, unfettered by national examinations, was an entirely new realm. This was what I had conjured in 1999 when I had designed my vision of education in the next millennia, a Liberalised Curriculum. To be able to transform what I had visualised some nine years before into reality was surreal. I loved every moment of that teaching stint and gave myself wholly to it.

To be able to transform what I had visualised some nine years before into reality was surreal. I loved every moment of that teaching stint and gave myself wholly to it.

These four years were also an eye opener in many ways. It was a time of much searching within. There were many moments of confusion, uncertainties and some controversies. I vividly recall an illustration made by the principal of the school then, that very often, decisions taken tend to swing like a pendulum from one extreme to the other. Time is needed for an equilibrium to be established. Another point he had made was that while it is ideal to start things well from the beginning, it is not possible to halt everything and start all over again. It is like boarding a train that is running and going along with it. I thought those were words of wisdom observed from real life.

There were many questions in my mind over many issues that I needed to delve deeper into, especially with respect to teachers embarking on the journey of curriculum planning. In search of answers to my questions, I pursued the Master of Education in

Gifted Education and chose the arduous path of doing a dissertation in place of coursework. I wanted to find out more about the experiences of teachers who were involved deeply in curriculum planning. To do so, I had to carry out the research on a larger scale by interviewing teachers from a spectrum of IP schools. I also decided to resign from my present school to maintain neutrality as a researcher. Through this research journey, I gained deeper insights into teaching, learning and how teachers impact curriculum. Thus, "Teachers as Curriculum Designers", my completed dissertation, was birthed.

In total, I interviewed eight teacher-curriculum designers working with high-ability learners (HALs) to examine the issue through a variety of lenses. The teachers who participated in my research had varied lengths of service (three to twenty years) and experience in curriculum work. They also differed in their subject disciplines and the number of IP schools they had taught in. I believe these variations allowed me to attain an understanding of the core experiences of teachers in writing IP curriculum, irrespective of their backgrounds and training.

When I embarked on the research in 2012, I could not find any published research study conducted in the area of curriculum design for IP schools. Subsequently, a research study examining the planning, implementation and enactment of a specific programme for HALs in an IP school was published in 2012.[5] Another study on school-based curriculum developers in the Language Arts in two IP schools was published in early 2014.[6] Nevertheless, there was still a dearth of studies examining the experiences and challenges of teachers across IP schools.

[5] *Taylor, Kwek, & Foo, 2011* [6]*Tay, 2013*

In the next two chapters, I will cover the key points of my research, re-written in retrospect as I integrate them with reflections of my own experience as an educator and curriculum designer. The people whom I anticipate to have an interest in this wealth of knowledge from the ground are the relevant policy-makers and school leadership, as it provides them with first-hand perspectives on the curriculum design journey. While the findings are by no means determinative, it is my hope that this richer understanding of curriculum designers' experiences, the contexts in which they operate and the struggles they face when carrying out their work, will inspire a deeper discussion of the issues faced. The tenets of curriculum design should be comprehensively considered for teacher education. This is particularly pertinent in today's landscape where more varied education paths are being availed to students, and greater autonomy is given to teachers in curriculum design.

APPENDIX

Model 1 The "family" of associated independent schools model each having a four-year programme for boys and for girls separately, culminating in a combined "junior college" programme at Years Five and Six offered by the Raffles family and the Hwa Chong family group of schools.

Model 2 The specialised school programme, namely NUS High School of Maths and Science with its own diploma, and the School of the Arts with the IB programme.

Model 3 The secondary school extended "upward" model which is offered by River Valley High School and Dunman High School.

Model 4 The junior college extended "downwards" six-year model offered by National Junior College and Temasek Junior College.

Model 5 The Anglo Chinese School (Independent) school and St Joseph Institution (Independent) six-year pre-IB and IB model.

Model 6 Two clusters of newly-associated secondary schools and junior college model, where Eunoia Junior College was the most recently established junior college in this category.

REFERENCES

Brooks, D. (2011). The Planning Fallacy. *The New York Times*. Available online at: https://www.nytimes.com/2011/09/16/opinion/brooks-the-planning-fallacy.html.

Gopinathan, S. & Deng, Z. (2006). Fostering school based curriculum development in the context of new educational initiatives in Singapore. *Planning & Changing*, 37(3), 93-110.

Kang, T. (2004). Taking human capital investment seriously: Reflections on educational reform. *Educational Research for Policy and Practice,* 3(1), 63-76. doi: http://dx.doi.org/10.1007/s10671-004-3932-y

Koh, E., Ponnusamy, L. D., Tan, L. S., Lee, S. S., & Ramos, M. E. (2014). A Singapore case study of curriculum innovation in the twenty-first century: Demands, tensions and deliberations. *The Asia-Pacific Education Researcher,* 23(4), 851-860. http://dx.doi.org/10.1007/s40299-014-0216-z

Ng, P. T. (2008). Educational reform in Singapore: from quantity to quality. *Educational Research for Policy and Practice,* 7(1), 5-15.

Tay, M. Y. (2013). *The ebb and flow of professional practice: case studies of language arts teachers as school-based curriculum developers in Singapore schools.* (Unpublished Doctoral Thesis), NIE, Singapore. Retrieved from http://hdl.handle.net/10497/14873

Taylor, P. G., Kwek, D., & Foo, A. (2011). *A study of the Raffles Programme at the Raffles Girls' School, Singapore.* Retrieved 24 April 2014, from National Institute of Education http://repository.nie.edu.sg/jspui/bitstream/10497/4442/1/NIE_research_brief_11-002.pdf

A chain is only as strong as its weakest link.

Thomas Reid

CHAPTER 6 TEACHERS AS CURRICULUM DESIGNERS: BUILDING THE SUPPORT SYSTEM

It is inevitable that at this point, my writing should take on an academic emphasis with some theoretical frameworks. It is through experience as a practitioner, that one realises that practical experience and observations needs to be constantly intertwined with that of understanding the concepts and tenets of educational theories, especially of those that had been built up by serious-minded educationists. Teachers attend training workshops which present a diluted version of these educational principles and are not presented with a strong foundation of the underlying issues that have been rigorously researched on. They therefore have a superficial grasp of these concepts and tenets, even whilst they may be inspired and excited by them.

The greatest irony of it all is, due to a lack of time, there is a lack of reflection which has led to the tendency to adopt ideas without a deep understanding of the educational outcomes which are intended or the limitations of the theoretical ideas they had been presented with. Another sad irony is, the conscientious teachers are often too exhausted to find time and energy to specially help a child in need when they have all the work on hand to infuse their teaching with what they had learnt from these workshops. How to strike a balance is an art that seems never to be mastered. Nevertheless, to ameliorate this situation, this chapter discusses the many facets I had gleaned through my research on curriculum design, which I hope readers will gain from as much as I did.

Multiple studies have shown that the design of a programme or curriculum plays a key role in affecting learners' outcome,[7] and that there are many reasons why school-based curriculum development makes sense. These reasons include seeing the school as a stable and enduring institution which is supposed to be more responsive to innovations and technologies in education,[8] or that educators within the school are the ones most aware of the needs of the students.[9] There are also teacher-centred reasons such as providing teachers with opportunities for self-actualisation, motivation and a sense of achievement,[10] as well as encouraging teacher-researchers in educational practices.[11]

...curriculum designing starts the minute the teacher begins conducting the lesson...

In Singapore, the responsibility for school-based curriculum design may fall on any teacher's shoulders. Curriculum designers have no fixed profile by years of experience, gender, or even job title.

[7] *Guskey, 2000; Barak, Ben-Chaim, & Uri, 2007*
[8] *Skilbeck, 1984; Bolstad, 2004*
[9] *Bolstad, 2004; Print, 1993*
[10] *Skilbeck, 1984*
[11] *Elliott, 1994; Stenhouse, 1988*

This is seen in the varied profiles of my interviewees and was also consistently expressed by them in our conversations. In fact, one of my research respondents perceptively stated that curriculum designing starts the minute the teacher begins conducting the lesson as every teacher has the autonomy to change the way of teaching a lesson.

> *"When a teacher goes into class, the first thing you say, the things you write on the board...that is curriculum. Whether you like it or not, the moment you step into class, the moment you mark a piece of work, you are actually doing curriculum work."*
>
> - F

How ready are our teachers to take on curriculum design work? All interviewees felt that teachers in Singapore would require at least a few years of teaching experience. Time is required for a teacher to properly comprehend the connection between the learning frame of their students and the curriculum, as well as to apply the appropriate pitching and teaching strategies. It is a big concern when inexperienced teachers are given the task of writing curriculum, especially without appropriate training support and time to assimilate the demands of the role.

As I dug deeper to learn about the journeys each of my interviewees had taken as a curriculum designer, I identified a compelling need for the development of teacher capacity in the specific role of curriculum design. In my research, the phrase "teacher capacity" refers to the following five broad sets of characteristics: teachers' knowledge, teachers' passion, teachers' beliefs about teaching and learning, teachers' reflectiveness and self-critique and teachers' disposition towards change.

IMPORTANCE OF TEACHER KNOWLEDGE

Teacher knowledge was cited by most respondents as an important factor affecting the effectiveness of curriculum designers. Shulman,[12] a renowned educational psychologist, identified three critical categories of knowledge that all teachers should possess: (1) subject matter content knowledge (2) pedagogical content knowledge (PCK) and (3) curricular knowledge. First, beyond knowledge of facts or concepts, content knowledge includes the ability to explain "why a particular proposition is deemed warranted, why it is worth knowing, and how it relates to other propositions."[13] Second. PCK refers to teaching strategies to bring about effective understanding. This includes knowing the variety of alternative forms of presenting the facts or concepts to students, knowing the areas where students would have difficulty, and knowing ways to address misconceptions. Third, curricular knowledge covers the "full range of programmes designed for the teaching of particular subjects and topics at a given level"[14] and understanding the characteristics of

Teacher knowledge was cited by most respondents as an important factor affecting the effectiveness of curriculum designers.

[12] 1986

[13] Shulman, 1986; p. 9

[14] Shulman, 1986; p.10

each circumstance where a distinct programme is being utilised. It includes familiarity with the curriculum materials of other subjects undertaken by the students at that level (lateral curriculum), and knowledge of the topics taught in the same subject area during the preceding and later years (vertical curriculum).

Naturally, competing definitions of teacher knowledge exist. There are definitions of curriculum knowledge[15] and teacher knowledge[16] which are quite broad. Nevertheless, teacher knowledge is viewed as the hallmark of teacher capacity.[17] One of my interviewees expressed the importance of school leaders providing direction in this respect. Having a specific curriculum model or curriculum theory which the whole school can adopt is a potentially effective way of guiding the process of curriculum design. Other interviewees pointed to the lack of basic understanding of curriculum design. Apart from the three very experienced teachers among my interviewees, a further three demonstrated a cursory knowledge of curricular approaches and curriculum development whilst two were not even aware of curriculum models! There is ample research on curriculum design, yet little has been done to tap on it.

VERTICAL AND LATERAL CURRICULUM

Consistent with Shulman's concept of "vertical curriculum", one of my interviewees felt that to be capable of designing a curriculum, the teacher had to have a level of curriculum competency that was higher than the level that he was designing for. For example, a teacher designing curriculum for Secondary Three, should possess curriculum competency of the subject matter up to Secondary Four

[15] *Zumwalt, 1989* [16] *Kang, 2004* [17] *McDiarmid & Clevenger-Bright, 2008*

and beyond. If the teacher only has competency at the equivalent level, he may not be able to fully evaluate the relevance of higher-order topics and assess whether they should be incorporated into the curriculum in response to changing trends. Perhaps this is especially pertinent considering that the IP is a substantial design endeavour for a six-year programme in which it is crucial that the curriculum designer be able to see how concepts are interlinked and build upon each other. Somewhat similar to the concept of "lateral curriculum" mentioned above, another interviewee advocated for familiarity with the different types of syllabi offered in Singapore schools as these are used as a reference for benchmarking. To her, familiarity with the GCE "O" and "A" Level syllabi was a minimum requisite for the task of curriculum writing.

> ***In many ways, I feel that the aspect of understanding HALs is often neglected, mainly because they are taken so much for granted and also because there is a misplaced belief that good students do not need to be taught.***

For the majority of the teachers who have been trained locally, their preparation to be an educator was often centered wholly on pedagogy. Most teachers embarking on curriculum design are therefore essentially dependent on their own teaching experience or in-house training courses, where available. Those who were in the school system when a new programme or pedagogy (such as IB, IP or UbD) was introduced, counted themselves fortunate as they benefitted from in-house training courses. These courses were discontinued after the transition phase however, and teachers who joined the school later were then expected to pick up curricular knowledge on their own.

UNDERSTANDING THE STUDENTS

In many ways, I feel that the aspect of understanding HALs is often neglected, mainly because they are taken so much for granted and also because there is a misplaced belief that good students do not need to be taught. Teachers tend to be confident they do know their students. It is also not uncommon to observe subjective judgments being passed, especially when teachers are overwhelmed by diverse responsibilities that cause a highly stressed environment. This is not helped by parents who, though well-intentioned for their children, impose their own viewpoints as well. Objectivity is a trait that is sadly deficient. What is needed to cultivate objectivity is both a science and an art.

It is paramount that teachers' understanding of curricular knowledge must extend to an understanding of their student learners as well. Some interviewees felt it was important to have a good understanding of students' abilities and characteristics in the spectrum of learners in order to determine the appropriate teaching strategies for various learner profiles. The research on HALs suggests that curriculum designers must be clear about the

[18] *Van Tassel-Baska & Stambaugh, 2006*

definition of curriculum,[18] the curriculum philosophy and the goals of the curriculum. The curriculum plan must also give attention to the progressive development of skills and concepts, and clearly specify the projects or alternative assessments. Other research focussing on the learning process of gifted learners have highlighted three key differences that distinguish these learners from others; i.e. their faster rate of learning,[19] their higher capacity and readiness to take on problem-finding and problem-solving,[20] and their higher capacity to grasp, connect and manipulate abstract concepts.[21]

...that it would be erroneous to paint the group of HALs with a broad brush. Teachers need to understand that even among HALs, students have asymmetrical learning abilities, which may affect how they deal with the curriculum...

All these are very im-portant tenets of curriculum planning that curriculum planners must possess. Hence, student learner characteristics must be one of the areas of focus.

GRADUATE AND PROFESSIONAL DEVELOPMENT COURSES

I wish to point out that it would be erroneous to paint the group of HALs with a broad brush. Teachers need to understand that even among HALs, students have asymmetrical learning abilities, which may affect how they deal with the curriculum in the classrooms.

[19] *Colangelo, Assouline, & Gross, 2004*
[20] *Rogers, 2007; Russo, 2004; Sternberg, 1985*
[21] *Gallagher & Gallagher, 1994*

Those interviewees who pursued a Master in Gifted Education believed it helped them develop a clearer and deeper understanding of HALs, which in turn aided them in their design of the curriculum. There is an interesting study on the difference in classroom practices between trained and untrained teachers of the gifted. It suggests that trained teachers, defined as those who have completed a minimum of four graduate courses in gifted education (GE), were more likely than untrained teachers to emphasise creative and thinking skills.[22]

Besides attending graduate courses, advocates for teacher development of those teaching gifted learners emphasise that the professional development of teachers is a critical and essential aspect of the GE programming.[23] In-depth teacher preparation, as well as regular and on-going professional development that stimulates desired practices are necessary.[24] Further research has suggested that intensive professional development programmes can (1) help teachers enrich their knowledge in their subject discipline, so that they can foster students' conceptual understanding; (2) increase teachers' awareness of student thinking; and (3) improve instructional strategies.[25]

In the same vein, GE teacher training appears to have been a significant source of support for my interviewees, even for those who did not personally participate in GE training. They explained that their curriculum designing process was enhanced through working on curriculum together with colleagues trained in the GEP. In some cases, the existing GE syllabus in their schools had been adapted from the GEP. In others, the teaching strategies used

[22] *Hansen and Feldhusen, 1994*
[23] *Gubbins, 2008; VanTassel-Baska & Johnsen, 2007*
[24] *Landrum, Callahan, & Shaklee, 2001; VanTassel-Baska & Stambaugh, 2006*
[25] *Borko, 2004*

in GE were applied in their schools. This phenomenon of drawing upon GEP training is also supported by two other local research studies.[26] In both these studies, the teacher participants attributed their confidence and expertise in their curriculum design work to their GE training. In a separate two-country study,[27] classroom observations of 31 Singapore teachers concluded that training experience strongly contributes to effective application of differentiated strategies when teaching GE classes. This consistent testimony regarding the robustness and benefits of the local GE training model suggests that it should be re-enacted in its fullness and disseminated to all schools.

Unfortunately, GE training has been greatly reduced to only one- to two-day workshops which barely scratch the surface of the topics. Half of the interviewees commented that the watered-down workshop is insufficient for a good foundation, whether in understanding the spectrum of learners or in planning and designing for this spectrum of learners. A lack of understanding of learners' traits can lead to misaligned curriculum design and teaching strategies. Indeed, a deep understanding of the characteristics of HALs is needed to plan for the development of their affective needs and character development. Workshops, professional sharing, and conferences are platforms that help teachers to grow and develop.

At this point, I must highlight that whether a programme is a structure of planned courses or an ad hoc amalgam of courses makes a difference. It has been observed that the core of every successful educational improvement effort is a thoughtful, well-conceived,

[26] *Leong et al., 2011; Tay, 2013* [27] *Van Tassel Baska et al., 2006* [28] *Guskey, 2000*

well designed and well supported[28] course.

COLLABORATIVE CURRICULUM DESIGN

While the discussion thus far has been focussed on the formal training of teachers, learning can also take place via peers, mentors or through dialogue with experts in the field. It has been observed that even when in-service programmes are conducted and attended, teachers may not apply the teaching strategies offered.[29] One of my interviewees said: "If you go on a course, you can come back, and people tell you that it won't work. Or you are told, you can't do it." How professional training can be translated into effective classroom practice is thus a concern. The same interviewee advocated strengthening social networks within the school system to improve teaching quality. Previous research substantiates this view that teacher involvement in a well-scaffolded collaborative design of curriculum materials has strong potential in deepening teachers' professional development as it provides the opportunity for teachers to share their professional knowledge and skills as well as reflect on their personal knowledge and beliefs, their practices and their goals for student learning.[30]

Leadership

In this respect, the role of the school leadership, school culture and school community cannot be ignored. When asked about an important source of support in the curriculum design journey, four interviewees described clear directives from the school leadership in terms of the outcomes expected of the curriculum. Another teacher expressed that the preparation of a teacher for the role should be done within the department by "reviewing what they

---

[29] *Barak et al., 2007*

[30] *Boldstad, 2004; Voogt et al., 2011*

have been doing in practice." This can then progress to seeing the bigger picture and understanding the features of curriculum design within a curriculum framework. To her, curriculum design was a progressive development, led ideally by the head of the department. Another interviewee also noted that heads of department played a key role in deciding how teacher capacity could be enhanced, yet different heads of department often exercised different levels of communication and involvement.

Peers

The presence of teamwork in terms of being able to get feedback and to discuss not only how to carry out the lessons, but also the level of difficulty in assessments and pitching of content was mentioned by all the interviewees as a key factor in supporting teachers in their curriculum design role. One of my interviewees was a strong advocate for developing a healthy school community which valued learning and sharing. She shared how her readings in her doctorate classes pointed to the need for a supportive culture within a school. There are invariably strong and weak teachers in any school, but a healthy sense of sharing and learning within the school community can

There are invariably strong and weak teachers in any school, but a healthy sense of sharing and learning within the school community can minimise these gaps.

minimise these gaps. Another interviewee reflected on the serious issue of the possible disenchantment of idealistic new teachers when faced with a school community which did not allow them to learn. While teachers wanting to learn can do so by attending courses and workshops, the biggest impact is felt in the "the day-to-day teaching... [and] marking." In her view, on-the-job learning matters as much, if not more, than formal courses.

Emphasising that there is more to the role of the social context in learning, an interviewee pointed out that there was a need for more peer collaboration as it was these interactions which made learning effective or ineffective. She emphasized that "the daily interactions in the community, for example, why it values this piece of work over that...will decide how the learning becomes entrenched within the teacher." How effectively teachers pick up skills is not just a cognitive transplant—it is the deliberate development of the *craft* of teaching. Hence, she felt that the school community should be considered when embarking on the IP. No amount of professional training can replace the environment of a school community. If schools combining to do IP do not have a shared culture and community, or this is non-existent at the point of inception, it is a concern.

Mentors

Apart from peer-learning, having experienced and good mentors has been identified by most teachers as a key support. One of them felt that good mentorship played a critical role in the development of teachers and accelerated learning for beginning teachers. He added that reflections and observations by good mentors help a teacher to pick up skills and be aware of "what is going on in the classroom." One of the interviewees was never part of any formal mentorship programme but considered one of her supervisors as her mentor. She was very grateful as she learnt how to see the big picture, and how to go about conceptualising and designing curriculum. She believes it is important for every teacher to have a role model or key figure to help lay some important foundational knowledge and provide guidance in values. This sentiment was echoed in another study which goes further to recommend that mentorship programmes should be maintained after the first two years of foundational professional development in GE.[31]

Back in the 1990s when schools were rapidly recruiting new GE teachers, a mentor from the GE branch was tasked to guide each teacher. The mentor was usually someone who had taught GE before and could guide the new teachers when there were issues. The mentor also acted as the coordinator among the teachers in different GE schools and helped in sourcing for materials to help the teachers prepare lesson materials. These informed new teachers of different pedagogical approaches and enabled them to teach beyond the scope of the syllabus.

These testimonies only serve to strengthen my suggestion that the model of more rigorous GE professional development and mentoring should be re-established. It is evidently an effective model that has clearly contributed substantially to teacher capacity, particularly in pedagogical strategies, even up to the present day and long after it has been phased out. Even if this model is not feasible due to the necessary expansion to a larger group of teachers, its key

[31] *Van Tassel Baska et al., 2006*

features, its criteria for selection of mentors, the effectiveness of the trainers and mentorship and the training programme should be woven into new professional development programmes. This could address the inadequacies of the current form of training, which the respondents in this study reported as piece-meal and lacking in impact. This teacher-training programme should also be extended beyond the teaching of HALs and include provisions for understanding curriculum philosophy and models to teachers teaching in mainstream schools. Researchers[32] have found that there is a need for teachers' professional learning to be differentiated and sensitised to context and career stage so that teachers can develop their competencies in the wide repertoire of pedagogical skill sets and feel efficacious later when their careers mature.

There is a wealth of teacher experience and teaching expertise that can and should be harnessed to build up a pool of mentors. The present intent to develop senior teachers, lead teachers and master teachers is commendable.[33] There are idealistic educators who entered the teaching profession at a time when the notion of a career path in teaching was unheard of. Their passion and drive to grow in educational expertise has made them the educators they are today. This dwindling pool of rich expertise should be quickly brought to bear in pressing areas of concern, one of which is the need for mentors to aspiring curriculum designers. Indeed, there are some teachers in IP schools who may not, for various reasons, have attained the titles of "lead teacher" or "master teacher" but who nonetheless possess immense expertise. Avenues to capitalise on such expertise should be developed, particularly the expertise of those who have

[32] *Sugrue, 2002, 2005*

[33] *MOE, 2014*

had the opportunity to participate in curriculum work, since they have navigated the transformations that have inundated the local education milieu. To lose this rich capital in human resource and talent would be a sad loss to our nation's education system. The need for mentors with curricular expertise to help teachers reflect and examine themselves in their role and scaffold their learning will lead to fruitful professional development and stronger school-based instructional leadership to support all teachers.

To lose this rich capital in human resource and talent would be a sad loss to our nation's education system.

Working with External Specialists

Beyond mentors, we should also look to specialists for support. One interviewee recounted inviting many specialists from the US and Israel to share what they did in their GE programmes. In one research study,[2] it was reported that some teacher participants were not aware of their lack of content knowledge until they worked in collaboration with experts. One particular interviewee described how the assignments and assessments crafted by the school were validated by experts in the field such as personnel from the College of William and Mary and the GE Branch in Singapore. She felt that this gave the teachers confidence in their role. Without this awareness, particularly of their own limitations, optimal professional growth may not be realised.

One interviewee felt curriculum experts need to have breadth of knowledge so that they would be able to prescribe the topics that would be more relevant. Classroom teachers who have taught for a long time may not have kept up with the current trends and may not question whether the syllabus is still relevant. This is where experts can come in to advise the teachers, who need to be involved as ultimately the teachers are the ones who know their learners well. The same teacher suggested that industrial attachments or secondments to research institutes would help teachers become familiar with current and future trends in the discipline. He reflected that "After teaching for some time, you tend to become oblivious to what are the essential skills that students require when they go out into the workforce because you get so used to the curriculum that you have been teaching. ... when you are bogged down by work, you tend to stop questioning the system."

CONCLUSION

Time is a scarce resource for all teachers. In terms of teachers working with gifted learners, studies have shown that pedagogies for teaching HALs are not applied due to the time needed to prepare students for high-stakes examinations.[34] It is ironic that the "universal" indicator of intellectual prowess can also serve as a possible obstacle in the curriculum planning and teaching of high-order cognitive thinking. In a Singapore IP schools study, the lack of time was one of the barriers for teachers who did not use the proposed teaching strategies for HALs.[35] Time is even more pressing for teacher-

[34] *Burke-Adams, 2007; Scot, Callahan, & Urquhart, 2009*

[35] *Slatter, 2009*

curriculum designers. The knowledge that needs to be acquired and applied in curriculum planning is expansive and the collaborative curriculum design model advocated in this chapter can also be very involved. Nevertheless, this is not an insurmountable problem if administrators take into account the requirements for curriculum planning in work-load allocation.

The knowledge that needs to be acquired and applied in curriculum planning is expansive and the collaborative curriculum design model advocated in this chapter can also be very involved.

It is also important to note that no education institution stands in isolation in a society. Research has cautioned against conferring roles based on ideological grounds or administrative convenience as "the school must apprehend its role in curriculum development as a close yet ever-changing partnership with other institutions and agencies in society. It does not make sense, to treat the school as the sole and exclusive determiner of the curriculum".[36] Schools must see themselves as a partner in the national education system and a member of the larger educational community, and vice versa.

[36] *Skilbeck, 1984; p2*

REFERENCES

Barak, M., Ben-Chaim, D., & Uri, Z. (2007). Purposely teaching for the promotion of higher-order thinking skills: A case of critical thinking. *Research in Science Education,* 37(4), 353-369. doi: 10.1007/s11165-006-9029-2

Bolstad, R. (2004). *School-based curriculum development: Redefining the term for New Zealand schools today and tomorrow.* Paper presented at the New Zealand Association of Research in Education (NZARE),24–26 November 2004, Wellington. http://www.nzcer.org.nz/pdfs/13514.pdf

Borko, H. (2004). Professional development and teacher learning Mapping the terrain. *Educational Researcher,* 33(8), 3-15.

Burke-Adams, A. (2007). The benefits of equalising standards and creativity: Discovering a balance in instruction. *Gifted Child Today,* 30(1), 58-63.

Colangelo, N., Assouline, S. G., & Gross, M. U. M. (2004). *A Nation deceived: How schools hold back America's brightest students.* Iowa City, IA: Belin-Blank Center.

Elliott, J. (1994). The teacher's role in curriculum development: an unresolved issue in English attempts at curriculum reform. *Curriculum Studies,* 2(1), 43 - 69.

Gallagher, J. & Gallagher, S. (1994). *Teaching the gifted child.* Boston: Allyn & Bacon.

Gubbins, J. E. (2008). Professional development. In J. Plucker & C. M. Callahan (Eds.), *Critical issues and practices in gifted education: What the research s ays* (pp. 535-562). Waco, Texas: Prufrock Press Inc.

Guskey, T. R. (2000). *Evaluating professional development.* Thousand Oaks, CA: Corwin Press.

Hansen, J. B. & Feldhusen, J. F. (1994). Comparison of trained and untrained teachers of gifted students. *Gifted Child Quarterly,* 38(3), 115-121. doi: 10.1177/001698629403800304

Kang, T. (2004). Taking human capital investment seriously: Reflections on educational reform. *Educational Research for Policy and Practice,* 3(1), 63-76. doi: http://dx.doi.org/10.1007/s10671-004-3932-y

Landrum, M., Callahan, C., & Shaklee, B. (2001). *Aiming for excellence: Gifted program standards, annotations to the NAGC pre-K-12 gifted program standards.* Waco. TX: Prufrock.

Leong, K. L., Sim, J. B.-Y., & Chua, S. H. (2011). School-based curriculum development in Singapore: Bottom-up perspectives of a top-down policy. *Curriculum Perspectives,* 31(1), 51-61.

McDiarmid, G. W. & Clevenger-Bright, M. (2008). Rethinking teacher capacity. In M. Cochran-Smith, S. Feiman-Nemser, D. J. McIntyre, & K. E. Demers (Eds.), *Handbook of research on teacher education: Enduring questions in changing contexts* (pp. 134-156). New York: Taylor Francis.

MOE. (2014). *Growing our teachers, building our nation.* Retrieved 25 April 2015, from http://www.moe.gov.sg/media/press/2014/09/growing-our-teachers-building-our-nation.php

Print, M. (1993). *Curriculum development and design.* NSW, Australia: Allen & Unwin.

Rogers, K. B. (2007). Lessons learned about educating the gifted and talented: A synthesis of the research on educational practice. *Gifted Child Quarterly,* 51(4), 382-396. doi: 10.1177/0016986207306324

Russo, C. F. (2004). A comparative study of creativity and cognitive problem-solving strategies of high-IQ and average students. *Gifted Child Quarterly,* 48(3), 179- 190.

Scot, T. P., Callahan, C. M., & Urquhart, J. (2009). Paint-by-number teachers and cookie-cutter students: The unintended effects of high-stakes testing on the education of gifted students. *Roeper Review,* 31(1), 40-52. doi: 10.1080/02783190802527364

Shulman, L. (1986). Those who understand: Knowledge growth in teaching. *Educational Researcher,* 15(2), 4-14.

Sie, S. H. (2015). *Teachers as curriculum designers for high ability learners: Perspectives, capacity and challenges* (Unpublished Master of Education Thesis), National Institute of Education, Singapore.

Skilbeck, M. (1984). *School-based curriculum development.* London: Harper & Row.

Slatter, C. J. (2009). *Teacher and student perceptions of critical and creative thinking within a science programme for high ability females in Singapore: Implications for classroom practice and staff development.* (Unpublished Master's Major Research Paper), National Institute of Education, Singapore.

Stenhouse, L. (1988). Artistry and teaching: The teacher as focus of research and development *Journal of Curriculum and Supervision,* 4(1), 43-51.

Sternberg, R. J. (1985). *Beyond IQ: A triarchic thoery of human intelligence.* New York: Cambridge University Press.

Sugrue, C. (2002). Irish teachers' experiences of professional learning: Implications for policy and practice. *Journal of In-Service Education,* 28(2), 311-338.

Sugrue, C. (2005). Rhetorics and realities of CPD across Europe: From cacophony towards coherence? In C. Day & J. Sachs (Eds.), *International handbook on the continuing professional development of teachers* (pp. 217-238). Maidenhead: Open University Press.

Tay, M. Y. (2013). *The ebb and flow of professional practice: case studies of language arts teachers as school-based curriculum developers in Singapore schools.* (Unpublished Doctoral Thesis), NIE, Singapore. Retrieved from http://hdl.handle.net/10497/14873

VanTassel-Baska, J. & Johnsen, S. K. (2007). Teacher education standards for the field of gifted education. *Gifted Child Quarterly,* 51(2), 182-205. doi: 10.1177/0016986207299880

VanTassel-Baska, J. & Stambaugh, T. (2006). *Comprehensive currciulum for gifted learners* (Third ed.). Boston, MA: Pearson.

VanTassel-Baska, J., MacFarlane, B., & Feng, X. M. A. (2006). A cross-cultural study of exemplary teaching: What do Singapore and the United States secondary gifted class teachers say? *Gifted and Talented International,* 21(2).

Voogt, J., Westbroek, H., Handelzalts, A., Walraven, A., McKenney, S., Pieters, J., & de Vries, B. (2011). Teacher learning in collaborative curriculum design. *Teaching and Teacher Education,* 27(8), 1235-1244. doi: 10.1016/j.tate.2011.07.003

Zumwalt, K. (1989). Beginning professional teachers: The need for a curricular vision of teaching. In M. C. Reynolds (Ed.), *Knowledge base for the beginning teachers* (pp. 173-184). Oxford, UK: Pergamon.

It is better to light a candle than curse the darkness.

William L. Watkinson

CHAPTER 7 TEACHERS AS CURRICULUM DESIGNERS: WHAT LIES WITHIN

I remember Dr Goh Keng Swee's passing on 14 May 2010. It was a poignant moment for me because he was a leader when I was a child and had been the chief architect of many of the policies which have shaped the education landscape in Singapore.

A team led by Dr Goh Keng Swee, then Deputy Prime Minister, had introduced streaming in 1980. I felt that it was discriminatory, especially since streaming would take place at a young age when the students would still be developing cognitively. I felt it was an unnecessary labelling of the students which would cause mental and psychological stress. The implementation of the programme was rigid, and some of the outcomes were not ideal.

Streaming at primary four was certainly a mistake, and has since been removed by then Minister of Education (1980-1981;

1985-1991), Dr Tony Tan. However, as I watched the Normal Academic and Normal Technical streams prove its efficacy over the years, albeit with many rounds of refinement, I saw that these indeed had a place in the education system. Overall, the system significantly improved not only the number of passes in the "O" Level examinations, but also mitigated the decline in attrition rates. This is clearly evidenced in the table below which presents the attrition rate of Primary 1 cohorts from 1976, shortly before the streaming policy was first introduced till recently.[37]

Percentage of P1 Cohort	1976	2002	2016
Eligible for Secondary School i.e. sat for the PSLE and qualified for Express, Normal (Academic/Technical) courses	67.5	98.5	98.3
Who had at least 5 N-Level passes or 3 O-Level passe	35.0	85.3	89.8

Statistics for the years before 2002 were not digitally available on the MOE website at the point of book printing.

The effectiveness of the introduction of the Normal Academic and Normal Technical streams had proven that Dr Goh Keng Swee and his team had indeed been visionary and far-sighted. Singapore's key resource is its human capital. The Normal Academic and Normal Technical streams have prepared our students according to their ability level, and ensured everyone would be able to contribute to the country. Time was needed for the system to prove itself.

[37] *Goh and Education Study Team, 1979; Ministry of Education, 2017*

I remembered feeling sad that such a significant leader, described by some as "the architect of Singapore's success", should not have been more honoured at his passing, at least at the school level. I noted school activities went on as usual and the event was just a passing moment.

Dr Goh often made mention of brilliance, character and values. I too, have been thinking about these qualities for some time now because, in the youths whom we are supposed to be nurturing, values are questioned and likewise, character: what is the worth of character against the abundance of new-generation distractions and gadgets? Brilliance is, of course, still important, since it raises one to an honoured pedestal. I am only thankful to have grown up in a better generation, built on nationhood and a care for the community (many thanks to my alma mater).

When I hear the way many kids today talk, I sometimes feel I have failed as an educator. I therefore hold dear this quote, that "It is better to light a candle than to curse the darkness." On my part, I know that example is better than precept. This chapter presents my research findings on inherent teacher capacity traits useful in the curriculum design process and how to enhance these traits. It is my hope that these findings will be able to light the path for teachers to become better curriculum designers, and therefore, better educators.

Teacher capacity is not a new concept. Other authors have used it to refer to teacher knowledge, craft skill, and teacher disposition.[38] In my research, the four inherent teacher capacity traits that emerged are teachers' passion, teachers' beliefs about teaching and

[38] *McDiarmid & Clevenger-Bright, 2008*

learning, teachers' reflectiveness and self-critique and teachers' disposition towards change.

TEACHERS' PASSION

Teaching is a demanding vocation. The outdated view of teaching as the mere transmission of knowledge has now shifted to one in which active thinking processes are encouraged. A teacher should become a thinking person himself to be a role model for his students,[39] and desire students to be able to apply complex reasoning skills even if the context of learning changes. Rote learning is no longer sufficient for students to thrive academically. In the same light, teachers need to understand and exhibit higher-order thinking processes, and have the ability to manipulate ideas with their students at the analysis, synthesis and evaluation levels.[40] On top of this, curriculum designers have added responsibilities that require a whole new knowledge and skill set.

> *A teacher should become a thinking person himself to be a role model for his students, and desire students to be able to apply complex reasoning skills even if the context of learning changes.*

There are however, some inherent qualities that appear advantageous in the curriculum design process. All the interviewees in my study cited the need for passion. They referred to

[39] *Furth & Wachs, 1974*

[40] *Barak et al., 2007; VanTassel-Baska & Stambaugh, 2006*

either a passion for the subject or a passion for enquiry and learning. With this passion to guide their way, they would do whatever was necessary to make their lessons meaningful, challenging and interesting for the students.

> *"I wanted the kids to love the subject...I did more than what was required. I was tasked with only resource packaging, but I came up with the whole book."*
>
> \- J

That teacher passion should have a positive effect on curriculum design is probably quite obvious. Two of the interviewees commented that IP schools also tended to attract a certain group of young teachers with the beliefs and dispositions that motivated them to constantly review and refine the curriculum to suit the needs of HALs.

With this passion to guide their way, they would do whatever was necessary to make their lessons meaningful, challenging and interesting for the students.

TEACHERS' BELIEFS ABOUT TEACHING AND LEARNING

Yet passion alone is hardly a sufficient condition for good curriculum design practices. To complement teachers' passion, some of the respondents were emphatic about teachers' beliefs being at the heart of their work in writing curriculum. I too, maintain that teachers must embody a set of beliefs that provide the principles for the planning and implementation of the curriculum. The approach to curriculum design should reflect not only these beliefs and principles, but also a value system and a clear grasp of the society and morality which form the foundation for these values and an understanding of the world. Some well-known approaches are Tyler's Rational-Linear Approach, Shwab's Practice of Deliberation and Eisner's Artistic Approach.[41]

Curriculum models are useful because they identify basic considerations needed in curriculum decisions and show their inter-relationships. In one research, the author listed as many as 34 models.[42] Such is the complexity of curriculum work. However, not all interviewees seemed to draw upon any curriculum model or curriculum philosophy. Only three of the more experienced teachers did so when explaining their curriculum design approaches. Separately and collectively, they mentioned socio-cognitive theory,[43] Shulman's Pedagogical Content Knowledge,[44] Shwab's Four Common Places of curriculum development,[45] Lave and Wenger's notion of community,[46] and John Dewey's Theory of Learning.[47] At the school

The approach to curriculum design should reflect not only these beliefs and principles, but also a value system and a clear grasp of the society and morality which form the foundation for these values and an understanding of the world.

[41] *Heng & Marsh, 2009* [42] *Marsh, 2009* [43] *Vygotsky, 1978* [44] *1986*
[45] *1978* [46] *Learning-Theories.com, 2014* [47] *1902*

level, only one teacher alluded to the adoption of a curriculum model in her school. This could explain the sad lack of attention to the application of curriculum models in the process of curriculum design.

TEACHERS' REFLECTIVENESS AND SELF-CRITIQUE

Building teacher capacity for more effective curriculum design extends to helping teachers develop a deep level of reflexivity and criticality. All the interviewees revealed a high degree of self-critique and reflection in the interview transcripts, in which they frequently asked themselves questions. This was especially evident when they talked about the concerns and challenges in their role. Even while responding to the researcher, they often openly questioned themselves, "Is there a better way to deliver?", "Did I meet learner's needs and ability?" or "How can I help students learn better?" Such deep capacity for reflexivity and self-criticality towards their curriculum design work and teaching and learning in general was observed in all the interviewees. For these teachers, their curriculum writing was significantly aided through conscious interrogation of their teaching techniques and observing the outcomes, or lack

For these teachers, their curriculum writing was significantly aided through conscious interrogation of their teaching techniques and observing the outcomes, or lack thereof. By doing so, they were constantly seeking to improve in their craft.

thereof. By doing so, they were constantly seeking to improve in their craft.

An experienced teacher can diagnose from the questions which students ask, whether any flawed reasoning exists in their understanding, and therefore whether (and how) their teaching technique can be improved. One of the interviewees rightly pointed out that these realisations do not occur suddenly. She explained that as the teacher progressed in his professional work, he would continue to analyse and question himself about what went wrong or what went right in the class. I must say this may not generally be the case, from most of my observations. There will always be many good reasons for justification but again if one wishes to reach the higher pedestal of an educator, some introspection on pedagogy is good.

The best teachers never assume they have arrived, but continually seek to refine their practice.

Some writers have pointed out that the quest to continually seek enhancement opportunities is the key to teachers' professional growth.[48] Without growth, teaching experience alone will not suffice. All teaching professionals need to re-examine their values, beliefs and trace their continuum of growth. The best teachers never assume they have arrived, but continually seek to refine their practice.[49] Just as we teachers would wish to inculcate independent self-directed learning skills in our students, we must ourselves possess them. It is only when this is done that collectively, a difference can be made for the new generation of learners.

[48] *Day, 1999; Hammerness, Darling-Hammond, & Bransford, 2005*

[49] *Kent, 2004*

"I do not have all the answers that are needed in education. Neither does MOE. Our schools have to think for themselves, and work collectively so that we nurture young Singaporeans who will ride the changes that will come into their lives in a more globalised world, and together create a bright future for Singapore."

- Shanmugaratnam, 2005

TEACHERS' DISPOSITION TOWARDS CHANGE

How does one start to plant the seeds of reflexivity and criticality? An open disposition towards change and learning certainly helps. In a cross-cultural study of teachers teaching the Gifted Programme in the United States and Singapore, teachers from both countries concurred that two of the main characteristics of exemplar teachers teaching HALs are having an open and flexible attitude in instruction methods, and being a lifelong learner.[50]

Similarly, openness to change and learning was found to be a factor that added to my interviewees' curriculum writing efforts. An interviewee felt that "experience is needed to extract [from] the abundance of resources, and teach it at the right level." Hence, learning from other experienced teachers is important.

That being said, experience can be a double-edged sword. Another interviewee learned that the tendency to fall back into old habits can be limiting, such as when teachers are absorbed in their old ways of teaching because that was the way they worked before. If teachers are not questioning the assumptions they hold, then they are most likely to brush aside any new theory or strategy that

[50] *VanTassel-Baska, MacFarlane, & Feng, 2006*

they are exposed to. Conversely, teachers need not be discouraged if experimental teaching activities do not work out. One interviewee learnt that if "certain things do not work out for one group of students, it may not fail with another group." She felt that teachers should focus on the present group of learners—what can be done for them—and not let past failures limit their experience.

PASSION FOR ENQUIRY

In my research journey, I had invited the interviewees to draw mindmaps of their curriculum design experience. Not only did this help them recall their thought processes, it also helped me visually understand their journey. What was interesting was how differently each interviewee perceived their journey and the focal point of curriculum design. Some interviewees' mindmaps were driven by their educational philosophy, some focussed on the variety of roles of the curriculum designer, while others featured the context of the design process such as high-stakes examinations and school management. The knowledge required of teachers is vast, and there is much for curriculum designers to educate themselves in.

The knowledge required of teachers is vast, and there is much for curriculum designers to educate themselves in.

The importance of having passion for enquiry thus became apparent to me. Interestingly, every single interviewee displayed this trait. They had all, on their own initiative, increased their capacity to understand and meet the demands and challenges of their multi-faceted role through reading and professional development. Most pursued higher degrees, such as a Master or PhD. Teaching experience did not seem to mitigate the need for more professional development. One of my more experienced interviewees felt inadequate as a curriculum designer despite having more than fifteen years of service in education, and embarked on her PhD in order to keep up with the latest research on curriculum design. While my sample size was small, I had been careful to ensure variability to ensure reliability; yet it may be more than just a coincidence that most of my interviewees have pursued higher degrees. It would be interesting to examine whether this drive to attain more knowledge at their own cost may be attributed to the lack of alternatives, such as more rigorous professional development or mentoring programmes.

THE ROLE OF RESEARCH

This quest for continual learning and improvement should not be limited to the individual level; it should really extend to the education industry at large. The observation by some authors[51] that there is visible diversity in Singapore secondary schools indicates the government's commitment to meet the diverse needs and profiles of students. More autonomy has been given through the many support structures and new initiatives which have been launched since the focus on ability-driven education began more than 15 years ago, with the aim of developing each child according to his potential.

[51] *Dimmock & Goh, 2011*

Today, school-based curriculum development is being conducted on the largest scale in the schools running the IP. However, even though this system-wide innovation and reform has been going on for some years, there is still a dearth of international prototypes, universal benchmarks or even empirical studies that policy-makers and educators can use.[52] At the very least, these would be useful to evaluate how far and how well such policy initiatives have fared in meeting their objectives. There is clearly an urgent need for more research-based studies, both to address any inadequacies as early as possible, as well as to pave the way for future innovations in education for the next generation of learners.

Well-designed and co-ordinated empirical studies need to be carried out on IP schools, and the findings of such studies should be shared on an open platform with the teaching fraternity. Learning from the failures and problems associated with each innovation or initiative is as important as learning from successful programmes. In times past, when changes were made to the curriculum and syllabi of each discipline, readily accessible documents to explain the rationale for the changes to educators did not exist. This is a huge disservice to the teaching fraternity as such documents and accounts can help teachers better understand curricular issues previously faced, drive greater urgency in the designing of a relevant curriculum and facilitate the development of deeper expertise. Without being able to learn lessons from what had taken place in the past, resources will be wasted each time a school embarks on curriculum design. History will inadvertently be repeated, albeit manifested differently.

[52] *Luke et al., 2005*

This is not the first time such observations and calls to action have been made.[53] IP utilises teacher-developed curriculum that involves the whole school and therefore can have a wider impact than other school-based curriculum development processes such as peer coaching or lesson reviews. Any shortcoming in the capacity of teachers to develop curriculum thus needs to be addressed with some urgency.

TIME

Given the multiple roles that teachers take in writing and implementing curriculum, as well as the complexities involved in curriculum design, there is an undeniable need for teachers to be supported by more time to help them in their curriculum writing efforts. This was echoed by all the teachers interviewed. In terms of teachers working with gifted learners, studies have shown that pedagogies for teaching HALs are not applied due to the time needed to prepare students for high-stakes examinations.[54] It is ironic that the almost universal indicator of intellect also serves as a possible obstacle in the curriculum planning and teaching of high-order cognitive thinking. In an IP schools study, the lack of time was one of the barriers to teachers using the proposed teaching strategies for HALs.[55] Time is even more pressing for teacher-curriculum designers. Instant results are impossible in curriculum design work. Nevertheless, this is not an insurmountable problem provided that administrators take into account the requirements for curriculum planning in work-load allocation.

[53] *Abdullah (2012); Leong et al (2011); Tay (2013)* [54] *Burke-Adams, 2007; Scot, Callahan, & Urquhart, 2009*
[55] *Slatter, 2009*

FINAL WORDS

In the light of globalisation and the knowledge-based economy, teachers in the forefront of curriculum design in IP schools need more support to acquire more than a surface understanding of the principles, ideology and vision in setting up IP curricula. They must be professionally trained in curriculum design. To develop the capacity of teachers in curriculum designing, purposeful planning is required for the professional development of teachers, targeted specifically at developing teachers' understanding of curriculum, curricular approaches, curriculum development and curriculum evaluation. This should include greater depth in the mastery of pedagogical content knowledge and breadth of curricula knowledge in the respective disciplines. A curriculum analysis approach to cultivate teacher thinking and judgement in curriculum work could be considered as an avenue for training.[56]

Indeed there is an urgent need to do so, especially with more innovative academic pathways for students emerging.[57] With every additional academic pathway and more teachers taking on different aspects of curriculum work with varying degrees of knowledge,

With every additional academic pathway and more teachers taking on different aspects of curriculum work with varying degrees of knowledge, planning for the development of teacher capacity in this area is vital.

[56] *Ariav, 1991* [57] *MOE, 2011*

planning for the development of teacher capacity in this area is vital. To enhance teacher professionalism, certification in the quality and competency of teachers in curriculum development should also be considered.

There also remains a need for a greater understanding of the impact of broad learning experiences versus the deep-seated examination-oriented culture that has dominated the local education framework. The purported intent of IP was precisely to answer the vision in "Thinking Schools, Learning Nation". In the words of then Prime Minister, Mr Goh Chok Tong,

> *"What is critical however is that we fire in our students a passion for learning, instead of studying for the sake of getting good grades in their examinations...It is the capacity to learn that will define excellence in future, not simply what our young achieve in school"*
>
> *- Goh, 1997*

Hence, life-long learning as an educational approach needs to co-exist purposefully with all other curricular concerns. By granting more autonomy and shifting the focus away from examinations, this ideology should have permeated the IP as the model of teaching and learning. Yet, curriculum leadership in this respect may not be sufficiently emphatic. Since space has been granted for systemic changes, the obstacles which remain could be in the mindsets of educators, school administrators and parents, and not merely attributable to structural change.

Finally, I would like to end with my thoughts about the schools' responsibility towards their students. I sincerely believe in the statement by the Education Minister then, Mr Heng Swee Keat, that "every school is a good school" in the sense that (as he clarified later) "every school can be a good school." Personally, I was surprised at the negative over-reactions to such a simple positive statement. "Good", by definition, includes what is positive, what is enhancing, what is developmental. It has nothing to do with status, ranking, the composition of the staff or student body or any of the other peripheral concerns that are not really of educational value.

To me, every school must embrace each student in his totality by accepting every child's strengths and weaknesses. Once a child is enrolled, the school should do its utmost to assess how each child can be developed, and actively work towards it. Whilst a system necessarily has criteria and standards to be met, some extra measures may be needed to help those students who experience difficulties. As mentioned in Chapter Three, the Principal of the full school that I taught at in the 1990s saw every child having a 10-year education in her school. She was addressing the school in the Direct School Admissions (DSA) exercise where she passionately appealed for colleagues to be vigilant and to remember that it was a child's life at stake. When we admit a student, the child must be regarded as

When we admit a student, the child must be regarded as ours to nurture to the end of the pathway in the school.

ours to nurture to the end of the pathway in the school. I make the same appeal. Every child matters. Whilst I agree that at some point of a child's life, there may be maladjustment or a lack of cognitive and affective readiness, I sincerely hope that despite the systemic constraints, there will be educators who will arise to do discrete good, and to remember to value every child. Every single child matters.

REFERENCES

Abdullah, D. (2012). *Exploring teacher professionalism: a case study of teachers' work in curriculum planning and development.* (Unpublished Masters's Thesis), National Institute of Education, Singapore. Retrieved from http://hdl.handle.net/10497/4724

Ariav, T. (1991). Growth in teachers' curriculum knowledge through the process of curriculum analysis. *Journal of Curriculum & Supervision,* 6(3), 183-200.

Barak, M., Ben-Chaim, D., & Uri, Z. (2007). Purposely teaching for the promotion of higher-order thinking skills: A case of critical thinking. *Research in Science Education, 37*(4), 353-369. doi: 10.1007/s11165-006-9029-2

Burke-Adams, A. (2007). The benefits of equalising standards and creativity: Discovering a balance in instruction. *Gifted Child Today,* 30(1), 58-63.

Day, C. (1999). *Developing teachers: The challenges of lifelong learning.* London: Falmer Press.

Dimmock, C., & Goh, J. W. P. (2011). Transformative pedagogy, leadership and school organisation for the twenty-first-century knowledge-based economy: the case of Singapore. *School Leadership & Management,* 31(3), 215-234. doi: 10.1080/13632434.2010.546106

Furth, H. G. & Wachs, H. (1974). *Thinking goes to school: Piaget's theory in practice.* Oxford, England: Oxford University Press.

Goh, K. S. & Education Study Team. (1979). Report on the Ministry of Education 1978. (pp. 1-3). Singapore: Singapore National Printers. Available online at: http://www.nas.gov.sg/archivesonline/speeches/record-details/7b01f369-115d-11e3-83d5-0050568939ad.

Hammerness, K., Darling-Hammond, L., & Bransford, J. D. (2005). How teachers learn and develop. In L. Darling-Hammond & J. D. Bransford (Eds.), *Preparing teachers for a changing world: What teachers should learn and be able to do* (pp. 358-389). San Francisco: Jossey-Bass.

Heng, M. A. & Marsh, C. J. (2009). Understanding middle leaders: a closer look at middle leadership in primary schools in Singapore. *Educational Studies (03055698), 35*(5), 525-536. doi: 10.1080/03055690902883863

Kent, A. M. (2004). Improving teacher quality through professional development. *Education,* 124(3), 427-435.

Learning-Theories.com. (2014). *Communities of practice (Lave and Wenger)* from http://www.learning-theories.com/communities-of-practice-lave-and-wenger.html

Leong, K. L., Sim, J. B.-Y., & Chua, S. H. (2011). School-based curriculum development in Singapore: Bottom-up perspectives of a top-down policy. *Curriculum Perspectives,* 31(1), 51-61.

Luke, A., Freebody, P., Lau, S., & Gopinathan, S. (2005). Towards research-based innovation and reform: Singapore schooling in transition. *Asia Pacific Journal of Education,* 25(1), 5 - 28.

McDiarmid, G. W., & Clevenger-Bright, M. (2008). Rethinking teacher capacity. In M. Cochran-Smith, S. Feiman-Nemser, D. J. McIntyre, & K. E. Demers (Eds.), *Handbook of research on teacher education: Enduring questions in changing contexts* (pp. 134-156). New York: Taylor Francis.

Ministry of Education. (2011, 18 November). *Implementation of Integrated Programme (IP) on track* from http://www.moe.gov.sg/media/press/2011/11/implementation-of-integrated-programme-on-track.php

Ministry of Education (2017). *Education Statistics Digest 2017.* Available online at: https://www.moe.gov.sg/docs/default-source/document/publications/education-statistics-digest/esd_2017.pdf.

Scot, T. P., Callahan, C. M., & Urquhart, J. (2009). Paint-by-number teachers and cookie-cutter students: The unintended effects of high-stakes testing on the education of gifted students. *Roeper Review,* 31(1), 40-52. doi: 10.1080/02783190802527364

Sie, S. H. (2015). *Teachers as curriculum designers for high ability learners: perspectives, capacity and challenges* (Unpublished Master of Education Thesis), National Institute of Education, Singapore.

Slatter, C. J. (2009). *Teacher and student perceptions of critical and creative thinking within a science programme for high ability females in Singapore: Implications for classroom practice and staff development.* (Unpublished Master's Major Research Paper), National Institute of Education, Singapore.

Tay, M. Y. (2013). *The ebb and flow of professional practice: case studies of language arts teachers as school-based curriculum developers in Singapore schools.* (Unpublished Doctoral Thesis), NIE, Singapore. Retrieved from http://hdl.handle.net/10497/14873

VanTassel-Baska, J. & Stambaugh, T. (2006). *Comprehensive currciulum for gifted learners* (Third ed.). Boston, MA: Pearson.

VanTassel-Baska, J., MacFarlane, B., & Feng, X. M. A. (2006). A cross-cultural study of exemplary teaching: What do Singapore and the United States secondary gifted class teachers say? *Gifted and Talented International,* 21(2).

Vygotsky, L. V. (1978). *Mind and society: The development of higher cognition.* Cambridge, MA: Harvard University Press.

There is one art of which every man should be a master–the art of reflection. If you are not a thinking man, to what purpose are you a man at all?

Samuel Taylor Coleridge

CHAPTER 8 REFLECTIONS

This is an extract from a blog post I wrote on 9 Feb 2014 when I embarked on a full-time Traditional Chinese Medicine (TCM) Advanced Diploma course conducted fully in Chinese by the Toa Payoh TCM College. The thoughts that I had noted then are relevant here.

扁鹊—DIFFERENCE IN VALUATION

"春秋战国时期，有位神医被尊为"医祖"，他就是"扁鹊"。一次，魏文王问扁鹊说："你们家兄弟三人，都精于医术，到底哪一位最好呢？"扁鹊答："长兄最好，中兄次之，我最差。"文王又问："那么为什么你最出名呢？"扁鹊答："长兄治病，是治病于病情发作之前，由于一般人不知道他事先能铲除病因，所以他的名气无法传出去；中兄治病，是治病于病情初起时，一般人以为他只能治轻微的小病，所以他的名气只及本乡里；而我是治病于病情严重之时，一般人都看到我在经脉上穿针管放血，在皮肤上敷药等大手术，所以以为我的医术高明，名气因此响遍全国。”

The above is an extract from an internet source. It is a story related by the TCM lecturer of a module called 医古文 (which means "medical historical literature") in the first lesson on 23 October 2013. The lecturer had actually referred to this quite early in the course, I think probably in early August, and it had left such a deep imprint in my mind that two months later, I looked it up.

(Incidentally, I think it is so necessary to learn things from the beginning, to look at historical perspectives of any given course or pathway, without which we would not be able to trace the cultural perspectives and its roots. This is also why I really enjoyed this module though it was in ancient Chinese, which I struggled to understand.)

扁鹊 was one of the famed physicians in Chinese medical history. The story recorded that once, the king asked him, "Among you and your two brothers, who is the best physician?" He replied that the best was the eldest, followed by his second brother and he was the least of them. Then the king asked, "Why then, are you the most famous?" He replied, "Eldest Brother treats an illness before it manifests itself, and because people do not realise that he had actually eliminated a potential illness, he is not highly regarded. Second Brother treats and cures illness at the initial stage, and because at that stage, people think that the illness is minor since he seemed to have cured it quickly, he is known only within the village. I treat illness at the critical stage, and I am seen treating wounds, using needles, letting of blood and so on, hence people regard my medical skills as brilliant.

The valuation of the masses versus the true valuation of a wise man of fame.

Whether the story is true or not, or whether the reasoning can be faulted or not—this is not my focal point.

Many of us are familiar with the breakdown woes of our Mass Rapid Transport (MRT) system in recent years. It is not my intent to join in the cynical camp that continually throws brickbats at the Singapore Mass Rapid Transit (SMRT) even as the breakdowns continually hit the headlines. However, it did cause me to think of the almost unproblematic running of the MRT in the early years when the rail system first started. I was very grateful for it, and for the foresight of those who had planned for it, at a time when the need was really questionable. Public transport has become many, many times more convenient since. People often do not realise that we owe it to those who really cared about their work, whose attitude was not, "I am paid only to do this", who went the extra mile, so that things run as well as they do for the relative ease and comfort in our lives today. This includes those around us—family members, friends, acquaintances—who have done more than their share, going beyond the call of duty. It is not just the "macro" planners who gave us the MRT. It is also people who consider the good of others first. Yes, these are the ones who think ahead, prepare, pre-empt, (I do

> ***These are not regarded even as heroes. Your conscientious ordinary folks are the reason for the welfare we have gained and now enjoy.***

not include those who are "kiasu", who look after themselves first) before a situation arises, yet who are often not recognised. These are not just unsung heroes. These are not regarded even as heroes. Your conscientious ordinary folks are the reason for the welfare we have gained and now enjoy.

The truth is, very often, the people who have had the foresight, consideration and thought to ensure that an event, a project or whatever programme is carried out smoothly, are often not as well regarded as the "heroes" in more dramatic situations. This includes those who take extra precautions like the people who ensure regular maintenance is carried out, who take steps to pre-empt accidents or who seek the positive growth of our children, etc. I can understand the discouragement and disillusionment that often dampen the spirits of those who may be overlooked for promotion or leadership simply because they are deemed as "not outstanding".

It is the ordinariness that far exceeds extraordinariness.

This is why the judgement of 扁鹊 is brilliant. If the story were a fable, the writer's perception is exceptional in recognising true value as opposed to ostentatious value. It is the ordinariness that far exceeds extraordinariness.

Another lesson I glean from this is the need to resolve a situation early and "treat" an issue at the initial stage. In the case of education, this is known as early intervention, when a problem is noted. It is true that when a problem becomes deeply rooted, it is sometimes much more difficult to eradicate.

This story had such a profound effect on me that it was a key reason for why I decided to return to the education field. At that time, I still intended to extend my knowledge, especially in Chinese herbs, but only as an interest, like music.

I was so sure of my calling to return to teaching that I wrote, "In fact, if I were to reflect upon the story of 扁鹊's brothers being better doctors than him because they were able to treat illnesses before they occurred or became worse, then it was clear that I should turn back to education. Every child that one can help, is likely to be one "better" adult." This was the email reply on 27 Nov 2013 which I gave to a good and valued friend who urged me to consider studying and practising TCM seriously, so that I could use it to benefit others.

I have to qualify however, that I do not equate education with "schools". It is not that I want to be a "better doctor". In actual fact, no one knows much about 扁鹊's brothers, who have remained nameless and were mentioned only because of the famous brother. This is precisely what I feel—that each and every person, with whatever talent one has, should contribute, without any regard for fame or achievement. For, what is achievement anyway?

The reason why I continue in this trend of thought is because of two conversations over the course of the second week of February in 2014. The first was with an acquaintance, with whom I had an unscheduled lunch. In relating how she and her family had settled in Singapore, she paused and acknowledged that it had been, in actual fact, very smooth. Having known and observed their circumstances for some time, I have noted that perhaps some things had been taken for granted by this acquaintance. Whilst sometimes there is an element of luck, most of the time, a lot of unseen preparations had been carried out in advance, which had not been recognised or acknowledged as effort. A pity.

Taking things for granted seems to be part of human nature, especially with people we are familiar. Cultivating an attitude of consideration and of valuing family members strengthens bonds. It is so easy to see the faults in others, especially when they are close to us. It takes wisdom to value each other's worth.

The second conversation took place after a steamboat dinner in my home with a few former students. The conversation turned to the negative comments appearing so often in social media. Although I personally would not waste my breath and time over these, some of them said that these remarks had made them aware of issues, and had made them think. While I concede that this might be true, I wish the awareness and thinking had come by more positive means. Inadvertently, the subject of "foreign talent" came up. Some of my best friends are among the so-called foreign talent and I am very proud of them. Honestly, this term means different things to different people, and arguments become very warped sometimes.

One grouse raised was that since these foreign talent were prepared to accept lower pay, they had "pushed down" wages. Another was that they were prepared to do extra, work overtime or carry out unpopular tasks, hence making locals look bad. Ironically, this was exactly the spirit of our forefathers who had come to this island—not being afraid of hard work and being prepared to endure hardships that have made our lives the richer now. Sadly, the question of fairness or unfairness to those paid lower wages for equal or more work done, was not an issue that was even considered.

I appreciate that these views were discussed openly. Whilst it was acknowledged that what I had raised at this dinner was true and right, the counter-argument given was that it is hard to accept, especially when "everyone is also saying the same", and it is easier to join the masses in their views. So, I was asked, what is the point of doing what is right when no one sees it nor appreciates it? I guess this brings me back again to the essence of the above story.

If one were to extend this analogy, it applies not only to being a physician. Wherever we are, if we can try to pre-empt, to be positive, to avoid fanning negativism or making "sores" worse, to do our part (however small and insignificant) to clear misconceptions (if possible), we would have fulfilled our role of being that unknown physician. We would be helping, in whatever small measure, not to propagate potential social ills, but rather, to alleviate it at the initial stage.

Thus, I feel that this simple story has so much to teach us— be a decent human being.

Does it matter who knows or not, or whether it is valued? The value lies in the act, however small, not in how others value it or whether it is even valued. For every protest of the futility of it all against the tide of the masses, I still say: "Each has to light his own candle and do his part". Alluding to others or pointing out the glaring injustices that may be true, I contend, does not mitigate one's own personal responsibility to another being, to humanity. Thus, I feel that this simple story has so much to teach us—be a decent human being.

On this simple note, I end my ruminations and reflections. This has been an unbelievable journey. I would never have thought I would be able to make it through this race course with all my wishes coming true.

Also, I would never have believed that it would actually be possible to achieve the completion of this book within the extremely tight timeline for this part of the race course. For years, I had wanted to write all these reflections and compile them into a book but many circumstances had prevented it. For this to have been possible, at this point, I wish to acknowledge two persons in particular.

The first person is, my all-time favourite educator and one-time principal, the one and only Miss Rosalind Heng of Singapore Chinese Girls' School (SCGS). I knew Miss Heng when she was an officer of the National Cadet Corps (NCC) of SCGS and I was an ardent supporter of CHIJ NCC as my sister was the Warrant Officer of the company there. SCGS and CHIJ had a close relationship and we were often placed in one another's care. A few years later, I had a tutee from SCGS and by then Miss Heng had assumed principalship of the school. I was stunned beyond words when I realised that this principal actually wrote remarks in each girl's report book! That left a deep impression on me.

Around September 1990 when I had intended to apply out of the school I was teaching in, a colleague who knew the Mathematics head of department at SCGS, helped to orchestrate an interview with the SCGS school administration. Honestly, I had no intention to join such a school as I had deemed SCGS an "elite" school. I was thus surprised at how simple the school was, and there was totally no showiness in the school. I was accepted into the school and remained there for ten good years. I remember the first prize-giving ceremony I attended at the school. It was just held in the school field with no elaborate speeches about achievements, etc. Despite the urgent need for funds to build a new school, there was never any pressure or compulsion to raise the funds through involuntary contributions on the part of students; teacher involvement in fund-raising was also minimal.

My greatest blessing in my teaching journey was to have worked under such a principal who had spurred me on to reach for self-actualisation in my own teaching vocation.

It was not what Miss Heng did. It was what she represented. I learnt so much from her as a person, as an educator. There were quite a few "scraps" that happened and the way she handled it with teachers, coaches, parents, students ... you had to be present to fully apprehend the largeness and wisdom of her heart. Usually, I would end up almost in tears, though I am not one who cries easily, being so touched by the love she showed towards her students and staff. She was always clear concerning who should be responsible; so if it was the child, the teacher should not bear the brunt of the matter.

Her integrity is priceless. Anyone coming to the school office asking how much to donate to get their child into the school never got anywhere. She refused any kind of gift; she made it known to the staff that she had declared it and paid for it, when once we (staff) had made the mistake of buying her an item for her birthday. My greatest blessing in my teaching journey was to have worked under such a principal who had spurred me on to reach for self-actualisation in my own teaching vocation.

For this, I dedicate this book to her.

The second person whom I wish to acknowledge with great gratitude is my friend, my former colleague, my fellow educator, my sister-in-Christ, Mrs Elaine Lim. Why she stood by me all these past thirty years, I will never understand. Whilst she was my peer in the University, we were acquaintances. When we became colleagues in SCGS, she was always the caring teacher who watched out for me because of my poor eating habits, was always the calming balm in my tumultuous times, and after I left the school, never failed to keep in touch and support me through the hardest of my circumstances. Through the arduous journey of writing my Master's dissertation, she was the one who supported me doggedly, editing and encouraging me to see it to its end. She somehow understood my compunction, my drive, my passion and my advocacy.

When I realised that time was literally running out for me and had given up thinking that it was even possible to get anything out for this book, she continued to plough through the dissertation to distill the essence, and somehow, helped to bring this work to fruition. Without her, without her sacrifices, without her firm belief and valuation of me, this would never have happened. The greatest virtue of this friend is her magnanimity of spirit, for being so determined to see her friend fulfil her sense of value without any thought for herself. She is a rare gem in this life; a friend by whom I have been truly blessed and I have been greatly privileged to have. Except to say thank you, dear friend, with the deepest of gratitude and appreciation, words entirely fail me.

Finally, to the fantastic editorial team, Daphne Yuan and Tan Siao Geng—who came out of nowhere since I actually had not even taught them at school—thank you so much for building the momentum to get things done within less than two months. I owe my thanks also to Sara Samantha Tan who stepped in to help with editing.

I also need to acknowledge three former students who have been indispensable during the writing stage of my dissertation: Wan Shen, Justin and Kenneth who gave me very strong administrative support to help me submit it on time. These are special students to whom I am bound by strong inner bonds which I treasure.

It is literally, for me, the end of the journey, and I am glad to say, it is a happy one. I hope the ruminations and reflections will evoke in each one who reads this, his own inward calling to answer and meet the needs of every child, to value each child and to make each one, a happy child.

I shall not live in vain.

Emily Dickinson

EPILOGUE

NOT IN VAIN

If I can stop one heart from breaking,
I shall not live in vain;
If I can ease one life the aching,
Or cool one pain,
Or help one fainting robin
Unto his nest again,
I shall not live in vain.
Emily Dickinson (1830–86)

不枉此生

若我能阻止一颗心被破碎
我将不枉此生
若我能减轻生命的心酸
或缓解疼痛
或安抚昏厥的知更鸟
回归它的温窝
我将不枉此生
艾米莉·迪金森 (1830–86)

1 Corinthians 13 King James Version (KJV)

4 Charity suffereth long, and is kind; charity envieth not; charity vaunteth not itself, is not puffed up,

5 Doth not behave itself unseemly, seeketh not her own, is not easily provoked, thinketh no evil;

6 Rejoiceth not in iniquity, but rejoiceth in the truth;

7 Beareth all things, believeth all things, hopeth all things, endureth all things.

8 Charity never faileth: but whether there be prophecies, they shall fail; whether there be tongues, they shall cease; whether there be knowledge, it shall vanish away.

DEVELOPMENT OF THE BOOK

It was somewhere between 2012 and 2015 that Siok Hui, who had been working on her Master of Education thesis, *Teachers as curriculum designers for high ability learners: perspectives, capacity and challenges,* expressed her wish to publish her dissertation findings.

Not long after, Siok Hui discovered that she had cancer. Despite being doubtful that the book could ever be written, with her innate love of a challenge and the strong encouragement of her long-time friend, Elaine Goh, she persevered with courage and fortitude. Serendipitously, help was forthcoming.

In the last six months of her life, Siok Hui was able to hold reunions with ex-students, from which four from Singapore Chinese Girls' School kindly volunteered to assist. Siok Hui and Elaine were joined by Daphne Yuan, Tan Siao Geng, Ang Jinglin and Corrine Ang. With their aid, Siok Hui was able to hold a mock-up of the finished book about a week before she passed away. It had been a joyful day for Siok Hui. Astoundingly, it had merely taken two months to complete. She had been in full control throughout—writing and editing as well as directing the artwork.

Throughout this journey, the team has constantly been amazed by the generous assistance of well-wishers, some of whom did not even know Siok Hui, but were moved by her story. The only desire of the team is that this book will inspire change and bring joy to others.

ABOUT SIE SIOK HUI

Sie Siok Hui, an educator for about 30 years, believed in nurturing the potential in every student because of her deep compassionate understanding of some of the emotional, social and academic challenges young Singaporeans face.

A local teaching scholarship recipient, she possessed a sharp analytical mind and was trained to teach secondary school Mathematics and English—an indication of her giftedness. As a teacher, she was exacting but students liked her witty lessons. The topic for her Master of Education thesis was inspired by her observations in the institutions she had taught in; few can match this diversity. These included government schools (Bedok Green Secondary School, Boon Lay Secondary School, Jurong West Secondary School and Nan Hua Secondary School), an autonomous school (Crescent Girls' School), independent schools (Anglo-Chinese School (Independent) and Singapore Chinese Girls' School), a specialist independent school (NUS High School of Mathematics and Science) as well as the National Institute of Education.

As her strength faded in the last two months of her life, Siok Hui drove herself to write and complete the book with an iron will and meticulous calibration of her medication. Given Singapore's small population size, hers is an urgent call for action to make changes for the sake of the future of the individual student as well as that of the country she dearly loved, her Singapore.

Siok Hui died on 1 November 2018, having led a purpose-driven and fulfilled life.